Contents

Map of FOCUS on PET				
UNIT	TOPICS	LEAD-IN	READING SKILLS	WRITING SKILLS
1	People Places Directions Friendships Relationships	Nationalities	*'A Child of the Forest'* Dictionary definitions Signs	Message
2	Homes Houses Family life Accommodation	Different kinds of homes	Labelling drawings Advertisements Notices *Debbie's letter*	Informal letter
3	Shops Shopping Services	Currencies and exchange rates	*Markets* Advertisements	Short report Message Ordering by post Town plan
4	Food Drink Restaurants	Picture puzzle Guessing game	Menu Letter Restaurant advertisements	Menus Questionnaire Short report Recipes Letter

5	Health
	Lifestyles
		Jokes
		Labelling parts of the
		  body
			Health
			'Lifestyles'
			'Reactivart'
				Notes during an
				  interview
				Daily routine
				Letter

6	Holidays
	Travel
	Hotels
	Weather
		Countries and capitals	Accommodation
			  advertisements
			Postcards
			'Inter-Rail'
				Booking
				  accommodation
				Postcards
				Fact sheet

7	Education
	Politics
	Language learning
		Matching people and
		  occupations
			'Travellers'
			Signs and notices
				Report based on
				  diagrams
				Questions
				Letter
				Expanding headlines

8	Entertainment Media Famous people	Visual puzzle Photographs of famous people	*'Capital Radio'* Advertisements Programme schedules *'Street Scene'* Headlines	Table Questions Booking form
9	Work Sports Hobbies Animals and pets	Cartoon Matching people and hobbies	*'Robin Knox-Johnson'* *'Dame Judi Dench'* *'James Warren'* Instructions	CV Letter

> FOCUS ON <

P·E·T

Preliminary English Test

DIANA L FRIED-BOOTH

Longman

		Map of FOCUS on PET		
LISTENING SKILLS	SPEAKING SKILLS	GRAMMAR	VOCABULARY	FURTHER PRACTICE and PET related Question
Class register Directions	Pairwork role-play – interview – directions	Reported speech	Family relationships	Writing (Part 2): Form filling Reported speech Writing (Part 3): Informal letter
Information sheet Matching visual information	Accommodation Preferences Planning a room Photograph	Uncountable nouns *there + be*	Buildings Signs	Reading (Part 1): Notices Writing (Part 3): Informal letter
Services and prices Table	Shopping habits Recommending shops	Instructions – zero conditionals *To have something done* *Need* + infinitive *Need* + gerund	Shops Services	Reading (Part 5): Gapped text Oral (Part 2): Role-play
Food bills Places to eat	Favourite food and drink Using a questionnaire	Adverbial order	Restaurant bill	Listening (Part 1): Mini-dialogues Writing (Part 3): Competition entry
Doctor's message *'Lifestyles'* Medical situations	Minor ailments Interviewing Role-play	Verb base + *-ing* *-ing* after certain verbs and prepositions	Major world religions Personal health/ hygiene	Reading (Part 1): Notices Reading (Part 3): Leaflet
Map route Notes	Planning a holiday	Passives Relative pronouns	Months of the year Seasons	Writing (Part 3): Letter Reading (Part 5): Gapped text
Notes from a telephone conversation Asking for help	Likes and dislikes – school subjects Photograph	Prepositions Modals – *must/mustn't/ ought to/should/ have to/don't have to*	Related vocabulary Dictionary definitions	Reading (Part 4): Extract Oral (Part 3): Describing a photo
Plans Booking form	Favourite programmes etc. Reasons for choices Making decisions	Phrasal verbs Imperatives	Theatres Tickets Entertainment	Listening (Part 2): Factual information Writing (Part 3): Video choices
Hobbies Sports report	Jobs Balloon debate Persuading people	Present perfect tense with certain adverbs and prepositions	Symbols Punctuation marks Abbreviations	Listening (Part 4): Dialogue Writing (Part 1): Transformations

1 People and Places

Lead-in

1 **Work with a partner. Look at these playing cards from a game called 'Happy Families'.**

- ☐ Where do these people come from ?
- ☐ What nationality are they ?
- ☐ What nationality are you ?
- ☐ Are there different nationalities in your class ?
- ☐ What nationality is your teacher ?

Master Oliveira
Brazilian

Mrs Kaur
Indian

Miss Nikolaidou
Greek

Mr Youssef
Algerian

2 **Look at these people. What nationality are they ? Use the jumbled letters to help you.**

NSSHAPI

PASEJEAN

AMIYSAALN

ISSSW

HFCRNE

AIATNLI

Listening

3 **You are going to hear a teacher talking to some new students at the beginning of a term. What do you think the teacher will ask the students? Look at the class register and fill in the missing information.**

CLASS 4				Jan. – Mar.
NAME	DoB	ADDRESS	PHONE NO.	NATIONALITY
Paco	29-11-72	15 Pentland	....	....
Rosa	....	....	....	....
Björn LARSEN	14-2-72	66 Cintra Avenue	53455	Swedish

Speaking and Writing

4 **Work with a partner.**

Student A You are the manager of Transworld Tours and you are looking for a person to work as Tourist Guide for your company. Use the form below to interview your partner.

Student B You want to work as Tourist Guide with Transworld Tours. The Manager has asked you to attend for an interview.

> **TRANSWORLD TOURS INTERVIEW FORM**
>
> Surname: ....
> First Name: ....
> Address: ....
> Nationality: ....
> D.o.B.: .... Tel.No.: ....
> School or College attended (with dates) ....
> ....
> Why do you want to work for Transworld? ....
> ....
> Language(s) spoken: ....
> Foreign countries visited: ....
> When can you start work? ....
> Brief statement on applicant's appearance: (eg. tidy, pleasant etc.)
> ....
> ....
> SIGNATURE .... DATE....................

For Further Practice in form-filling see page 116.

Reading

5   **Before you read the text 'A Child of the Forest' answer these questions.**

☐   Who wrote this article ?
☐   What is the title of this article ?
☐   How old is the writer of this article ?

6   **Look at the map. Can you guess where Gloucestershire is ?**
Read these dictionary definitions; they explain some difficult words in the text.

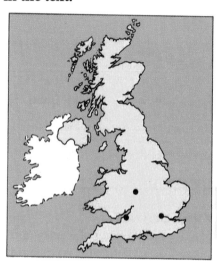

gutter /gʌtə/, **gutters** ...A gutter is... **1.2** a plastic or metal channel fixed to the lower edge of the roof of a building, which rain water drains into.

tell off. If you **tell** someone **off**, you speak to them angrily or seriously as a way of punishing them for doing something wrong.

maiden name, maiden names. A woman's **maiden name** is the surname she had before she got married and took her husband's surname.

7   **Now read the article and answer the questions. If you agree put a tick (✓) under Yes; if you disagree put a tick (✓) under No.**

		Yes	No
1	The book was written 70 years ago.	____	____
2	The book has appeared in translation.	____	____
3	Winifred Foley came from a large family.	____	____
4	Winifred Foley has a lot of childhood photographs.	____	____
5	Winifred Foley was glad to leave school.	____	____
6	She still lives in the same area where she grew up.	____	____

8   **Read the text below and fill in the spaces using *one* word only.**

Winifred Foley's family was very poor. They (1) .... in a small cottage (2) .... Gloucestershire. She (3) .... seven brothers and sisters but three died in early childhood. When she was young she had (4) .... sleep with two of her sisters (5) .... was very uncomfortable.

When she grew (6) .... she wanted to be a dancer and a singer (7) .... she knew she could not because she had to go into domestic service.

When she (8) .... school she was sad. (9) .... she was not very good (10) .... mathematics she liked reading and writing.

A child of the forest

by Anna Vaughan, 10

Anna interviewing author Winifred Foley

A FRIEND of my family, David Goodland, is writing a play based on **A Child in the Forest**, a famous book by Winifred Foley.

The story is set in the Forest of Dean, Gloucestershire, and is about her growing up 70 years ago in a mining family.

The book sold over half a million copies all over the world in all sorts of different languages.

Her family was very poor and their cottage was very small. Winifred Foley had seven brothers and sisters but three died in early childhood. She now has three sisters and one brother. When she was young she had to sleep with two of her sisters and her brother and it was very uncomfortable. Her baby sister slept in her parents' room. Her Aunt Lizzie also lived with them so it was very hard.

Winifred Foley had her school photograph taken in 1925. A photograph was rarely taken so it was quite a big event.

When she grew up she wanted to be a dancer and a singer but she knew she could not because she had to go to work.

When she had to leave school she was sad. Although she was not very good at mathematics she liked reading and writing.

She married Syd Foley, but before she was married her maiden name was Mason. She did not write her first book until she was 61, but **A Child in the Forest** was a huge success.

Her hobbies are gardening and painting and she also likes music like Beethoven's **Pastoral Symphony**, because it reminds her of birds, flowers and mainly walking through the forest.

One thing that she remembers when she was a child is sitting under a roof gutter and letting the water drip on her head, and she always got told off.

She now lives in a cottage in the Forest of Dean with her husband.

She is very excited about seeing her childhood acted out on stage, and said that it was something beyond her wildest dreams.

Grammar

▶   **REPORTED SPEECH**

9   **Work with a partner. Look at these questions:**

Where did you live when you were a child, Mrs Foley ?
Did you have any brothers or sisters ?

**What other questions do you think Anna wrote down to ask Mrs Foley ?
Write down four, and then check these with your partner.**

10   **Imagine Mrs Foley asked Anna a question.**

Mrs Foley: What do you want to be when you grow up, Anna ?
Anna: I want to be a newspaper reporter or a journalist.

Mrs Foley's question and Anna's reply would be reported like this.

Mrs Foley asked Anna what she wanted to be when she grew up.
Anna said she wanted to be a newspaper reporter or a journalist.

11   **Ask your partner *one* of these questions.**

What do you want to be when you leave school/college ?
What did you want to be when you were a child ?

Tell your teacher what your partner answered. For example:

Jean-Luc said he wanted to be a pilot.

12   **Look at the way sentences can be changed when you want to
report what a person has said.**

a   'How many books have you sold ?' Anna asked Mrs Foley.
     Anna asked Mrs Foley how many books she had sold.
b   'When did you leave school ?' asked Anna.
     Anna asked when Mrs Foley had left school.
c   'What are your hobbies ?' Anna said.
     Anna asked Mrs Foley what her hobbies were.
d   'Do you want to be a writer ?' Mrs Foley asked Anna.
     Mrs Foley asked Anna if/whether she wanted to be a writer ?

13   **Write your own grammar rules for reported speech.**

For Further Practice turn to page 117.

**Listening
and Speaking**

14 **Listen to the recording. Look at Map A below and see if you can follow the directions you hear.**

15 **Work with a partner.**

Student A (Close your book.) You want to get to The Albany Hotel.
Student B (Look at Map B.) You are a clerk in the Tourist Information Office in Upper Parliament Street.

16 **Now change roles.**

Student A (Look at Map C.) You are a clerk in the Tourist Information Office in Clarence Street.
Student B (Close your book.) You want to get to Queens Hotel.

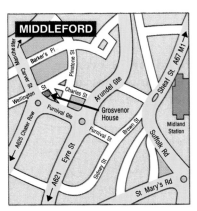

Map A

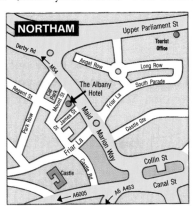

Map B

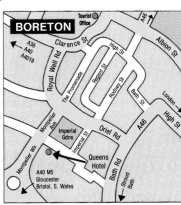

Map C

Reading

17 **Where might you see these signs ?**

1

2

3

4

18 **What is the purpose of sign 1 ?**

☐ to signal the start of the roadworks
☐ to tell drivers where to deliver goods
☐ to apologise for any inconvenience
☐ to explain the reason for digging

Writing

19 Anna has forgotten her door key. Look at the message she's left for her mother.

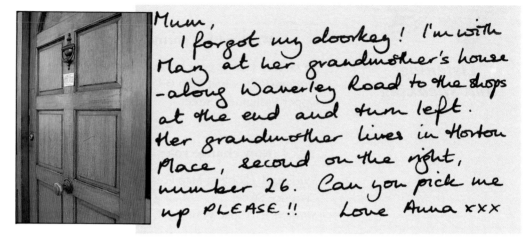

> Mum,
> I forgot my doorkey! I'm with Mary at her grandmother's house - along Waverley Road to the shops at the end and turn left. Her grandmother lives in Horton Place, second on the right, number 26. Can you pick me up PLEASE!! Love Anna xxx

20 Imagine you have gone out with your friend for the evening. Leave a message saying where you have gone. Exchange messages with your partner. Write a short reply to your partner's note. For example:

> Okay! Have a good time.

> See you!

> Hope you enjoyed yourself. Am in bed - ASLEEP!

> What about me!

> See you tomorrow.

21 Look at this leaflet. You want to visit Beaulieu. Write a message to your friend suggesting you meet to discuss the idea. Tell her/him why you want to go.

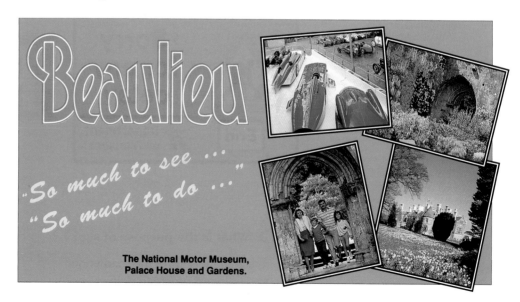

Beaulieu

"So much to see ..."
"So much to do ..."

The National Motor Museum,
Palace House and Gardens.

For Further Practice turn to page 117.

KNOW YOUR VOCABULARY

22 Use the following words to describe Jan's relationships within his family. Label the boxes. (One has been done to help you.) Be ready to explain these relationships to your teacher.

brother / sister / father / uncle / aunt / grandfather / grandmother / cousin

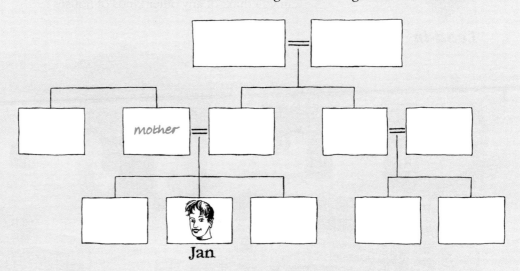

23 Match the numbers with the letters. One has been done for you.

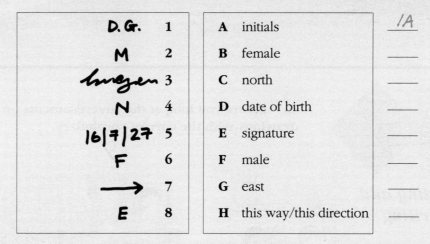

D.G. 1	A initials	/A
M 2	B female	___
(signature) 3	C north	___
N 4	D date of birth	___
16/7/27 5	E signature	___
F 6	F male	___
→ 7	G east	___
E 8	H this way/this direction	___

24 Learn these words. Listen to your teacher and mark the main word stresses.

For example: córner

1 married	**4** nationality	**7** niece	**10** square
2 single	**5** husband	**8** nephew	**11** junction
3 relative	**6** wife	**9** crossing	**12** crossroads

2 Homes

Lead-in

1 **Look at these different kinds of houses. Ask your partner:**

☐ Would you find houses like these in your country ? If not, why not ?

☐ Would you like to live in any of these houses ? Why or why not ?

☐ Can you think of any other kinds of houses ?

Reading and Writing

2 **Before you look at the advertisements on the next page, match the drawings with the correct vocabulary.**

lounge
double-glazed
fitted kitchen
bungalow
carpet
kitchen/diner
utility room

3   Now look at these advertisements for accommodation. The language used in advertisements is often shortened to save space and money. Can you find any examples in these advertisements of how this is done?

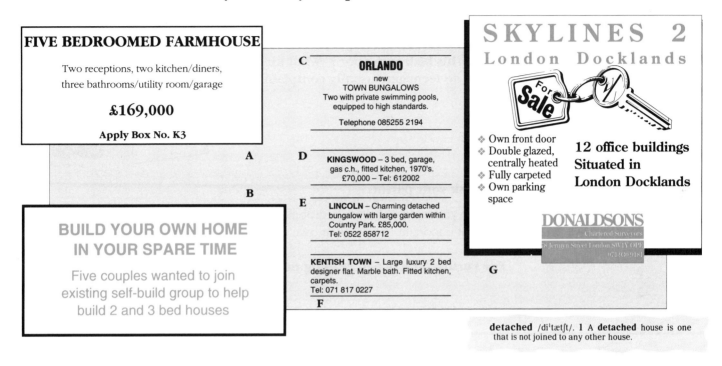

FIVE BEDROOMED FARMHOUSE

Two receptions, two kitchen/diners, three bathrooms/utility room/garage

£169,000

Apply Box No. K3

A

B

C   **ORLANDO**
new
TOWN BUNGALOWS
Two with private swimming pools, equipped to high standards.

Telephone 085255 2194

D   **KINGSWOOD** – 3 bed, garage, gas c.h., fitted kitchen, 1970's.
£70,000 – Tel: 612002

E   **LINCOLN** – Charming detached bungalow with large garden within Country Park. £85,000.
Tel: 0522 858712

KENTISH TOWN – Large luxury 2 bed designer flat. Marble bath. Fitted kitchen, carpets.
Tel: 071 817 0227

F

SKYLINES 2
London Docklands

For Sale

❖ Own front door
❖ Double glazed, centrally heated
❖ Fully carpeted
❖ Own parking space

12 office buildings Situated in London Docklands

DONALDSONS
Chartered Surveyors
8 Jermyn Street London SW1Y 0PE
071 930 9181

G

BUILD YOUR OWN HOME IN YOUR SPARE TIME

Five couples wanted to join existing self-build group to help build 2 and 3 bed houses

detached /dɪˈtætʃt/. 1 A **detached** house is one that is not joined to any other house.

4   The people below are looking for some kind of accommodation. Read what they want. Which advertisement would you recommend each of them to reply to?

Susan and Tom don't have much money but they have plenty of time!

Mrs Jackson doesn't want to live in a town. She doesn't like flats and finds stairs difficult to climb.

Ms Blum is looking for new business accommodation with somewhere to leave her car.

Mr Miles would like a family house with a garage and central heating.

5   Ask your partner what kind of accommodation he/she would like. Write down a description of the accommodation your partner wants.

Reading

6 Look at this cartoon.
Do you find it funny ?

7 Why has the child put these notices
on her/his bedroom door ? What kind of
things do teenagers usually complain about ?

'But I'm your mother
and I just want
to dust your room.'

8 Ask your partner:

☐ Do you have your own bedroom or do you share a room ?
☐ Is it important to have your own room ? Why or why not ?

For Further Practice in reading notices turn to page 118.

Reading

9 Read the letter below which was written by a girl called Debbie.

I really feel like leaving home but I'm only fifteen. My mum and dad
are so strict they won't let me do any of the things my friends do.
For example, on a Saturday evening everyone goes to the disco but
my parents say I have to be home by nine o'clock and the disco
doesn't finish until twelve. It's really unfair and everyone laughs at
me and calls me a baby.

Also my mum goes into my bedroom when I'm at school and I'm
sure she looks through my things. When I ask her not to she says it's
not my house and I'm too young to have a private life.

They treat me as if I'm still a child and won't trust me to do things
on my own. I want to get a job on a Saturday but they say I have to
do homework, then help look after my younger brother. If they
won't change I'm going to run away and then they'll be sorry...

10 Do you think you would find this letter in:

☐ a book ?   ☐ a diary ?   ☐ a magazine ?   ☐ a comic ?

11   **Now answer questions 1-6. If you agree put a tick (✓) under True; if you disagree put a tick under False.**

		True	*False*
1	Debbie has left home.	____	____
2	The disco finishes at midnight.	____	____
3	Debbie's friends make fun of her.	____	____
4	Debbie's mother thinks her daughter needs privacy.	____	____
5	Debbie has a weekend job.	____	____
6	Debbie's letter is full of complaints.	____	____

12   **Work with a partner. Try to decide why Debbie wrote this letter. If you were Debbie's friend would you do anything to help her ? What advice would you want to give Debbie's mother and father ?**

Speaking and Writing

13   **Ask your partner where he/she lives:**

Do you live in a house / bungalow / flat / apartment ?
(Note that 'apartment' is American English for 'flat'.)

14   **Look at the pictures below. Ask your partner where he/she would prefer to live and why.**

15   **Write down one good reason for living in:**

- ☐ a flat
- ☐ a house
- ☐ the centre of a city
- ☐ a suburb
- ☐ a town
- ☐ a village
- ☐ the country

Listening

16 You will hear two people talking to an estate agent about the kind of accommodation they would like. As you listen fill in the information sheet below. Some of the information has been filled in for you.

HOUSEFINDERS Agency

NAME ......STOPES.........................MR/MRS/MISS/MS

Tel. No. (daytime) ....

___

House ☐   Flat/Apartment ☐

Rent ☐   price ....
Buy ☑   price ....

Number of rooms ....

___

Furnished ☐   Unfurnished ☐

___

Central heating ☐   Shower ☐

Garage/parking space ☐   Laundry room ☐

Position ....

....

....

HOUSEFINDERS Agency

NAME ....MR/MRS/MISS/MS

Tel. No. (daytime) ....

___

House ☐   Flat/Apartment ☐

Rent ☐   price ....
Buy ☐   price ....

Number of rooms ....

___

Furnished ☐   Unfurnished ☐

___

Central heating ☐   Shower ☐

Garage/parking space ☐   Laundry room ☐

Position ....

....

....

Grammar

▶ **UNCOUNTABLE NOUNS**

17 **Look at the following list of nouns. You can *never* use 'a' or 'an' with these words. Are these words** uncountable **in your own language ? Can these words be made *plural* ?**

money / furniture / traffic / countryside / transport / scenery / information / accommodation / news

18 **Complete the sentences below by choosing one of the words above to fill each gap.**

1   Have you heard the .... about John - he's getting married !
2   When I move into my house I'm hoping to buy some new ....
3   The house is situated in the .... surrounded by the most beautiful
     ....
4   Can you lend me some .... until I get paid on Friday please ?
5   The government is building another motorway which should stop some of the heavy .... going through the city centre.
6   Cheap .... in London is difficult to find and some students have to live at home or stay with friends.
7   If you haven't got a car you have to use public .... such as buses and trains.
8   If you want some .... about hotels in the UK you should write to one of the tourist offices.

▶ **THERE + BE**

19 **Look at the sentences below. It is possible to rewrite each example using** there + is **or** there + are**. Work with your partner to complete the gaps.**

1   Some newspapers have accommodation advertisements.
     There .... accommmodation advertisements in some newspapers.

2   This apartment has two bedrooms.
     .... two bedrooms in this apartment.

3   Estate agents have lots of information on houses and flats.
     There .... lots of information on houses and flats with estate agents.

4   My flat has central heating.
     .... central heating in my flat.

5   Each house has four bedrooms and a study.
     .... four bedrooms and a study in each house.

Speaking

20 Many people, especially students, live in what is called a 'bedsit'. This is short for 'bedsitter'. You usually have to sleep and eat in the one room and share a bathroom and toilet.

Do you have this kind of accommodation in your country ? What do you think are the advantages and disadvantages of a bedsitter ?

21 Look at this plan of a room. Decide with your partner how you would furnish this room. What colour would you paint it ? Where would you put the furniture ?

Writing

22   **Imagine you are studying abroad and the room opposite is your bedsit. Write a letter to an English-speaking friend telling them about your room. The letter has been started for you. Write another 60 words.**

> Dear ....
>
> I arrived here safely but the journey took almost twenty-four hours so I was really tired. The college is great and I think I'm going to enjoy the course.
>
> But I must tell you about my room. I've got a room in a large house; there are three other students in the house as well and we all share the bathroom. Anyway, my room is really nice. It's ....
> ....

For Further Practice turn to page 119.

Speaking

23   **Work with a partner.**

Student A   Look at the photograph on page 123.
Student B   Look at the photograph on page 132.

Don't let your partner see your photograph !

Ask each other about your photographs. Once you have a rough idea about your partner's photograph try and draw (very approximately !) what you think it looks like.

Listening

24 **Work with a partner. You will hear people talking very briefly about different things. As you listen, look at the groups of pictures below numbered 1-5 and decide which picture in each group correctly describes what they are talking about.**

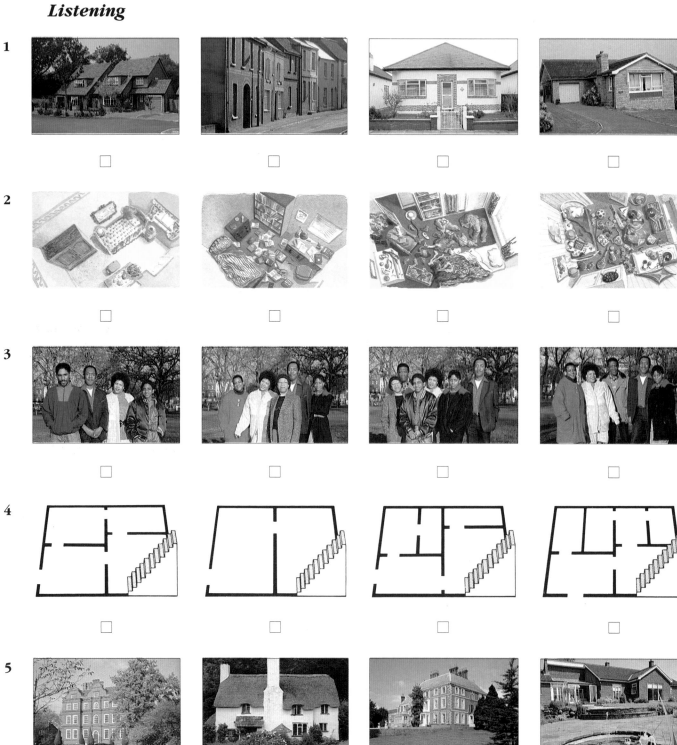

KNOW YOUR VOCABULARY

25 **Label the building. Use these words to help you.**

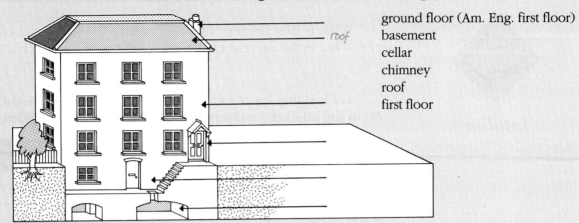

ground floor (Am. Eng. first floor)
basement
cellar
chimney
roof
first floor

roof

26 **Learn these words. Listen to your teacher and mark the main word stresses.**

For example: building

1 upstairs	**6** cupboard	**10** elevator (Am. Eng.)
2 downstairs	**7** living room	**11** inhabitant
3 bookcase	**8** bungalow	**12** lavatory
4 kitchen	**9** apartment	**13** escalator
5 dining room		

27 **What's the difference in meaning between these two signs ?**

28 **Where would you expect to see these signs ?**

3 Shopping

Lead-in

1 What is the currency in your country? What currencies can you think of? What is the current exchange rate of your currency with the US dollar?

2 Look at this list of exchange rates. As you listen to the financial report fill in the missing numbers. Some have already been filled in for you.

Bureau de Change

Rates per £1		We Buy	We Sell
Australia $		2.33	2.14
Austria Sch		16.59	
Belgium Fr.			44.77
Canada $			
Finland Mkk		7.62	
France Fr.		8.28	7.63
Germany Dm.			2.17
Greece Dr.			
Holland Gld		3.25	2.99

3 Work with your partner. Look at the coins below. How many do you recognise?

Look at the list. Can you rearrange the letters to make countries, and then match each country with its currency?

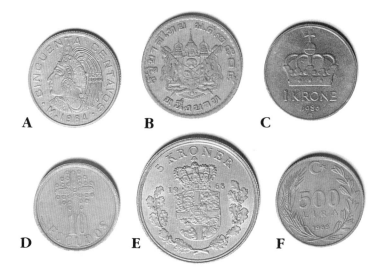

A   B   C

D   E   F

1	YTREKU	3	RLGPOATU	5	LHDAIANT
2	KDREAMN	4	XOCEIM	6	WRANYO

Speaking

4   **Work with your partner. How many different kinds of shops can you think of ?**

5   **You want to find out about your friends' shopping habits. Copy these questions onto a sheet of paper to make a short questionnaire.**

1   How often do you go shopping ?
2   Do you have a favourite kind of shop ?
3   How much money do you spend on yourself every week ?
4   What sort of things do you spend your money on ?
5   Where do you prefer to shop: in a market or in a department store ?

Shopping Habits Questionnaire	Maria	Björn
How often do you go shopping?	twice a week	once a week - always on a Saturday
Do you have a favourite kind of shop?	yes- music/ record/ hi-fi shops	
How much money do you spend on yourself every week?		
What sort of things do you spend your money on ?		
Where do you prefer to shop: department store or market?		

Put your questions to other students in the class and write down their answers.

Writing

6   **You now have the information to write a short report on your friends' shopping habits. Organise your answer by writing one or two sentences on each question. Use the ideas below to help you.**

☐   I interviewed .... people in my class about their shopping habits. Most of them go shopping once a day/at the weekend/two or three times a week.

☐   They like many different kinds of shops. Five people said that clothes shops/ boutiques are their favourite places although other people …

☐   Some people have more money to spend than others. For example, … They spend their money on different things. All of them spend money on sweets each week but …

☐   Finally, most people prefer to shop in department stores because … /
☐   Lastly, not many people prefer to shop in a market because … / although three people think a market is best for fresh fruit and flowers.

Reading

7 **Read the two texts on markets. Then work with a partner and answer questions 1-5.**

A

Every day is market day in Hong Kong. The Chinese housewife is so insistent on fresh food that she will go to market not just once - but twice a day to make sure her family has the very best.

The Chinese have a great variety of green vegetables which are known to be not just good for people but also good for the soil. So Chinese markets have a much larger variety of green vegetables than anything else. There will also be many different types of fruit (most of it imported), along with thousands of ducks which arrive daily in Hong Kong from mainland China, and many varieties of fish.

B

Leeds market, in the north of England, was built in 1857. Part of the market is still very traditional and sells coloured sweets, biscuits, jewellery, materials and china. But there are other new sections to the market which sell cheap toys, music cassettes and plastic shoes.

You can also buy cheap food, fruit and vegetables and some of the best bread to be had anywhere. In one corner it is even possible to buy a simple meal and (if you don't mind the noise) to sit and watch everything going on around you for hours on end.

If you agree with a statement put a tick (✓) under Yes; if you disagree put a tick under No.

		Yes	*No*
1	Both markets sell vegetables.	____	____
2	Both markets sell fish.	____	____
3	Chinese women expect to shop more than once a day.	____	____
4	Leeds market is small and quiet.	____	____
5	Food seems more important in the Hong Kong market than the Leeds market.	____	____

For Further Practice in reading turn to page 120.

Listening

8 **You will hear some tourists in the UK asking about different services. Work with your partner and try to guess where each tourist is likely to be.**

9 **Look at the goods in the shop window. You will hear the same tourists asking about the cost of different things. Put a tick (✓) against each thing you hear, and write down the cost.**

pen
Price ....

pencils
Price ....

jacket
Price ....

coat
Price ....

watch
Price ....

camera
Price ....

bottle opener
Price ....

sweater
Price ....

tie
Price ....

tin opener
Price ....

For Further Practice in talking about what to buy, turn to page 121.

Grammar

▶ **INSTRUCTIONS**

10 **Both these sentences express a possibility followed by an instruction to do something.**

1 If you smell gas - call the Gas Board.
2 If your new shoes leak - take them back to the shop.

11 **The following sentences are incomplete. Can you suggest how to finish them, using the examples above to help you ?**

1 If you need to buy a stamp - ....
2 If you want to get some petrol - ....
3 ...:.. - go to a bank.
4 .... - ring the police station.
5 If you don't want to go shopping - ....

▶ **HAVE SOMETHING DONE**

12 Look at these examples of how we ask to have something done

1 I want to have my watch mended.
2 I want to have (*or* get) my trousers cleaned.

Use the following cues to write similar sentences.

3 car / repair
I want ....
4 Jane's car / clean
Jane wants ....
5 children's shoes / heel
The children want ....

▶ **NEED**

13 Need can be used in two ways:

1 I need to write a letter.   active   need + to (infinitive)
2 My eyes need testing.   passive   need + -ing (gerund)

Notice that 2 can also be expressed like this and still mean the same:

I need to have my eyes tested.

In 1 the sentence means *you have to do something*.
In 2 the sentences mean that *something needs to be done*.

14 Make sentences from the following cues using the above examples to help you.

1 My / passport / renewing
2 Rosa / needs / have / photo / taken
3 I / need / buy / suitcase
4 Our / house / painting

5 David needs / phone / brother
6 Dan's / bike / repairing
7 The police / need / catch / thief
8 I / need / have / teeth / checked

Reading

15 Read the page of advertisements opposite. Try and answer the following questions.

1 What are the makers of Floral shampoo offering ?
2 Where can you shop late ?
3 What should you do if you smell gas ?
4 How long does the Art Sale last ?
5 What is special at Stokes today ?
6 Where can you go if you want to insure your luggage when going abroad ?
7 What kind of information will you get if you phone 76565 ?
8 What is Helene offering ?

A

Twells plc
Bristol

MONDAYS	Closed
Tuesday	9.00am-6.00pm
Wednesday	9.00am-6.00pm
Thursday	9.00am-8.00pm
Friday	9.00am-6.00pm
Saturday	9.00am-6.00pm

LATE NIGHT SHOPPING
We are open for late night
shopping every Thursday until
8.00pm throughout the year.

B

OLD MILL CARPETS
CARPET CLEARANCE SALE
3 DAYS ONLY - ALL MUST GO!
FRIDAY-SATURDAY AND SUNDAY
9th, 10th and 11th FEBRUARY
DON'T MISS IT!!

OLD MILL CARPETS, MARKET STREET, WELLS
Telephone WELLS (0749) 76565

C

SPECIAL TODAY
CLASS 1
CANARY
TOMATOES
29p lb

STOKES

D

Thomas Cook

Travel
insurance

E

British Gas
IMPORTANT
If you smell gas, or think you
have a gas escape, call us
immediately. You will find our
number listed under "Gas" in
the phone book.

F

COUPON WORTH
15p OFF
NEW SHAMPOO FLORAL

G

SALE **MASSIVE** SALE
ART SALE
ONE DAY ONLY - Sunday, February 4th
10.30 am - 5 pm
at
The Mendip Lodge Hotel, Frome

OVER 100 PAINTINGS BEING SOLD AT RIDICULOUS PRICE OF ONLY £10 EACH!

H

FREE DRY CLEANING
Do you like to keep
your clothes clean
and looking smart? If
so, why not become
a "Mystery Shopper"
and have some of
them cleaned for
free! *For further
details telephone*:
Helene on
071-863 7755
(office hours)

16 **Look at the advertisement G. Imagine you went to the sale and
bought a picture. Write a few sentences about your picture saying why
you chose it.**

Writing

Writing

17 Look at this page from a mail order catalogue. Using this service you can buy things through the post. Choose one thing for yourself and something different for a friend. Fill in the order form.

PARKER PEN SET
A duo of fountain pen and ball-point
in a stylish matt blue finish, gift boxed.
**Parker Pen Set
£25.00**

WALLET
A slim, black wallet, crafted from fine leather, embellished with distinctive red stripe suitable for ladies or gentlemen.
Wallet £15.00

**COMPACT DISCS
£11.00**

**NECKLACE
£30.00**

Mail Order Catalogue

PRODUCT DESCRIPTION	PRICE

FOR YOU (please print)	FOR A FRIEND (please print)
NAME	NAME
ADDRESS	ADDRESS
COUNTRY	COUNTRY
POST CODE/ZIP	POST CODE/ZIP
DAYTIME TEL:	DAYTIME TEL:

NAME:	(please print)
SIGNATURE:	DATE:

Listening

18 You will hear a city guide talking to some tourists who are being shown around a shopping precinct. They are on the first level listening to his introduction. Work with a partner and fill in the table by putting a tick - like this (✔) - in the correct box.

Shopping Precinct

LEVEL	1	2	3
cafe/bar			
shoes			
dried flowers			
gardens			
souvenirs/gifts			
clothes			
postal service			
chocolate			

*Speaking
and Writing*

19 Work with your partner. Write down some of the shops in your town or the area where you live.
Has your town/area got everything ? Is there anything else you would like to see such as new shops or services ?

20 If you were asked to recommend some of the best shops to a foreigner, which would you suggest ?
Draw a plan of your town/area and mark six of the best shops. For example, the best food shop, the most fashionable boutique, a shop which sells traditional goods etc.

21 Imagine you have to leave this information for a visitor. Write a few lines saying why you have chosen these particular shops.

KNOW YOUR VOCABULARY

22 **The signs over the shops in the High Street are missing. Add the sign to each shop.**

23 **Look at these pictures and answer the questions.**

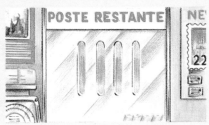

1 If you post your letter now, when will the postman collect it ?

2 Can you use the telephone ? Why not ?

3 Why is it useful for tourists to know about Poste Restante ?

24 **Learn these words. Listen to your teacher and mark the main word stresses.**

For example: currency

1	electricity	**4**	telephone	**7**	weight	**10**	customer
2	self-service	**5**	operator	**8**	market	**11**	account
3	souvenir	**6**	borrow	**9**	shop assistant	**12**	dial

4 Food and Drink

Lead-in

1 **Work with a partner and look at the picture puzzles below.**

Spot the Sweet
These sweets may all *look* the same, but one is different. Which one is it?

Count the Sweets
Take a quick look at this page and then try to guess how many sweets are in the jar. No counting!

2 **Look at this shopping bag. Your partner has been shopping for food and drink. What do you think she/he has bought ? Write down your ideas without showing your partner.**
   Now check each other's lists !

Listening

3 Look at the bill for Mrs King's shopping. How many things did she buy ? How much was the total bill ? Did she pay with the exact money or did she get some change ?

4 Now listen to the conversation between Mrs King and the girl who does her shopping for her. As you listen try to fill in the missing figures on the bill.

```
              J SAINSBURY PLC
                   BATH
        TELEPHONE NO. 0225 444737

                            £
    SQUEEZY HONEY          0.
    JS HALF FAT MILK       0.
    JS CORNFLAKES          0.
    JS HOVIS LOAF          0.53
    LEMON TEA BAGS
    NEW POTATOES
    JS FILTER COFFEE
  BANANAS
  1.40 lb @ £0.56/lb       0.
  TOMATOES
  0.18 lb @ £0.95/lb       0.17
  CARROTS
  1.20 lb @ £0.29/lb       0.
    HALF CUCUMBER
    CAULIFLOWER            0.

    BAL DUE                7.66

  CASH                     8.00
  CHANGE                   0.34

  005 17 141 6008 10:01 23MAR96

   THANK YOU FOR YOUR CUSTOM
   PLEASE RETAIN THIS RECEIPT IN
       CASE OF ANY QUERY
```

Reading

5 Menus in the UK are often written in three parts. If a menu is described as a 'three-course menu' it means:

a starter - for example soup, fruit juice or paté, followed by:
a main course - usually a choice of fish or meat, followed by:
a dessert (often called 'pudding'), for example ice cream, fruit salad and/or cheese.

Coffee can be included in the price of the meal but it is usually extra.

6 **Work with a partner and look at this menu from The State House restaurant. Use a dictionary to look up words you don't know.**

<u>MENU</u>

CHILLED FRUIT JUICES

FRENCH ONION SOUP

EGG MAYONNAISE

LONGSHIPS PATE SERVED WITH HOT TOAST AND A SIDE SALAD

****

ROAST CHICKEN WITH BACON AND SEASONING

GRILLED FILLET OF PLAICE GARNISHED WITH PRAWNS, MUSHROOM
AND LEMON

PANFRIED SIRLOIN OF STEAK SERVED WITH A CREAM, BLUE CHEESE
AND A PORT SAUCE

HAM OMELETTE

****

A SELECTION OF STEAKS AVAILABLE ...
FILLET 7 OZ   SIRLOIN 8 OZ   T BONE 16 OZ
(PRE COOKED WEIGHT AND AT A £2.50 SUPPLEMENT)

****

A SELECTION OF FRESH SEASONAL VEGETABLES

****

A SELECTION OF SWEETS

****

COFFEE AND DINNER MINTS

****

£17.50

****

THE CHEF WILL BE HAPPY TO PREPARE ANY OF YOUR FAVOURITE
DISHES WITH 24 HOURS NOTICE.

The State House
LAND'S END

☐ How many starters are there ?
☐ What can you choose for a main dish ?
☐ Do you have to pay extra for coffee ?
☐ How much is the cost of a meal ?

Writing

7 Imagine that you have been asked to write out a typical menu for English-speaking visitors to your country.

When you write out your menu, you may need to explain what some dishes are. For example a visitor to Switzerland who sees Rösti on a menu will not necessarily know that this is a potato dish. Don't forget to add the prices !

Speaking

8 What is your favourite food ? What is your favourite drink ? Do you have a favourite meal ?

Now find five people who agree with your choices and five who disagree.

Reading

9 Read the text below and answer the questions.

and we spent the rest of the day just lying on the beach. In the evening, however, we went to a restaurant recommended in one of the tourist guides. It was fantastic ! The food was excellent and so was the service. Surprisingly it was not very expensive and the waiters were really friendly. I couldn't decide what to have - there was such a choice ! Anyway in the end I had grilled chicken with various vegetables followed by the most delicious ice cream. Gerd had a seafood salad with lots of different fish including pieces of raw fish which we'd never had before. For dessert she had coconut ice cream – actually served in half a coconut shell – which is very smooth and creamy. I'm going to try and make it when we get back. If you haven't planned where to go for your holiday why not come here ? I'm sure you'd both love it. There's plenty to do and I can certainly recommend where to eat...

1 What do you think this text comes from?
2 What do you think the writer is trying to do?
3 What are the things the writer likes about the restaurant?
4 What is the writer planning to do when she returns?
5 What suggestions does the writer make?
6 Why would somebody read this text?

Listening

10 Listen to these people deciding where to eat. Match the person(s) with their chosen place by writing a letter in the box below each picture.

3 ☐

1 ☐

4 ☐

2 ☐

5 ☐

For Further Practice in listening turn to page 122.

Grammar

▶ **ADVERBS**

11 **Look at these sentences.**

Jonathan cooks very well.
I like rice dishes best although I like pasta too.
I dislike cabbage and I don't like carrots either.

The adverb in these sentences goes at the end of the sentence.

Rearrange the following sentences with the adverb at the end.

1   homework very Michael well his did
2   the too come I can café to ?

12   It is usual to keep a verb and its object together, so an adverb should not normally separate them. For example:

I like eating out in restaurants very much.   *or*
I very much like eating out in restaurants.

I don't like cooking for myself very much.   *or*
I don't very much like cooking for myself.

Rearrange the following sentences making sure that you don't separate the verb from its object.

1   very reading books I much cookery like
2   of heavy don't bags I carrying shopping like much

13   Most adverbs go before a verb, but after the verb to be. For example:

Victoria often visits her uncle's bakery.   *but*
Victoria is often in the café with her friends.

Robert never goes to a restaurant.   *but*
Robert was never good at cooking.

Rearrange the following sentences taking care to put the adverb in the right place.

1   our on we do Saturday often shopping a
2   happy am to friends I always my cook for

14   When there is more than one part to the verb, for example 'have cooked', 'should be boiled', then the adverb usually goes after the first part. For example:

I have never cooked a meal in my life !
River water should always be boiled before drinking.

Rearrange the following sentences taking care to put the adverb in the right place.

1   always farm local fresh I bought have eggs from my
2   liked have coffee night at I drinking never late
3   cake if out will keep never the of oven the you taking rise it
4   ever you raw eaten have fish ?

Reading

15 **Look at these advertisements for places to eat in the south of England.**

The Four Seasons Restaurant

Enjoy our beautiful oak panelled Restaurant in the heart of Salisbury.

A candlelit dinner for two starts at around £10 - £12 per person. Enjoy our superb 4 course Sunday lunch at only £5.95.
12 Rooms available
Price Range from £20 up to £46 per night. Half board rates include evening meal, from £30 per night per person.

WEEKEND BREAK - Special price: prices on request.

The White Horse Hotel
38 Castle Street, Salisbury, Wiltshire SP1 3RJ.
Telephone: (0722) 27844

"Fine food and wine at affordable prices"

CAFÉ MATISSE
Opening Hours
9am - 11pm Monday to Saturday
7pm - 10.30pm Sunday

Café Matisse
4 Drury Street, Winchester. Tel: 0962 69630

Eating Out
IN
SALISBURY
&
WINCHESTER

The
Rajpoot
TANDOORI RESTAURANT

Our food is prepared in a style which blends the finest oriental spices to produce a variety of subtle and exotic flavours without over spicing.

140, FISHERTON ST. SALISBURY

2 minutes from central car park
1 minute from railway station
For table reservations phone:
Salisbury (0722) 334795

The Cricketers

Bar Food & Meals.
Inn Accommodation,
Garden & Play Area
for children.

5 Bridge Street,
Winchester, S023 8HN.
Telephone: 62603

Authentic
Italian/American
Pizza
Call! - we deliver free.

Restaurant at:
12 Upper High Street
Winchester.
Telephone: 840384

Work with a partner and ask each other the following questions.

1   How many days a week is the Café Matisse open ?
2   Which restaurant advertises a four-course meal ?
3   Can you park outside the Rajpoot ?
4   Which restaurant can I phone to have food brought to my home ?
5   Which restaurant is suitable for parents with a young family ?

**Speaking
and Writing**

16   Now use the questionnaire below to interview at least five other students in your class about their eating habits. Copy the questions onto a separate sheet of paper first.

Use the following scores for each persons's answer:
Yes, often = 3   Sometimes = 2   Hardly ever = 1   No, never = 0

1. Do you think you eat too much?

2. Do you eat snacks like biscuits, nuts, chocolate?

3. Do you drink fizzy drinks like Coca Cola or Pepsi Cola?

4. Do you enjoy eating foods like crisps, chips and peanuts?

HOW DID THEY SCORE?

9 or more	5-8	0-4
Perhaps these people are eating too much of the wrong kind of food?	Perhaps these people are careful over what they eat?	Are these people going hungry?!

17   You should now have enough information to write a brief report (about 60 words) about some of your friends' eating habits. Your teacher will help you.

**Speaking
and Writing**

18   Look at the recipe below for Mixed Pepper Salad.

MIXED PEPPER SALAD
1 Lollo Rosso
1 medium red, green and yellow pepper
2 oranges
small cucumber
sunflower oil, 25ml (1fl.oz)
vinegar 50ml (2fl.oz)
apple juice
5ml (1 teaspoon) clear honey

Line dish with Lollo Rosso.
De-seed peppers and slice into thin strips.
Peel and slice oranges.
Mix all ingredients together.

Your teacher has been asked to put together some of your favourite recipes for a class of students in the UK. With a partner discuss a recipe for something which you know how to make. It must be easy to prepare. Decide on the ingredients and then write out the recipe. Pass your recipe to another pair of students and ask them to check it for you.

For Further Practice in writing turn to page 123.

ingredient /ɪnˈgriːdɪənt/, **ingredients. 1 Ingredients** are the things that are used to make something, for example all the different foods you use when you are cooking a particular dish.

Writing

19   **An English language magazine is organising a competition. The prize is a weekend for two at the Cherry Tree Hotel in Liverpool in the north of England with all costs paid.**

You have to write a letter (not more than 80 words) to the editor of the magazine which includes the following points:

- ☐ the length of time you have been learning English
- ☐ your reasons for learning English
- ☐ whether you have visited any other countries
- ☐ who you would take with you if you won
- ☐ why you would like to win the weekend

Use the information below to help you, and start your letter 'Dear Editor,'.

WIN A WEEKEND FOR 2 IN LIVERPOOL!

CHERRY TREE HOTEL

FRIDAY
Arrive at your leisure
7.00 pm - 9.00 pm
Dinner in the Restaurant.

SATURDAY
7.30 am - 9.30 am
A leisurely full English Breakfast.
Morning at leisure. Visit the famous
Northern Market and shop for bargains.
Tour the beautiful countryside.
7.00 pm - 9.00 pm
Gala Dinner in the Restaurant.

SUNDAY
8.00 - 10.00 am
English Breakfast.
An opportunity to visit the
magnificent, world-famous Cathedral.
This afternoon take a guided tour
of the beautiful city
7.00 - 9.00 pm
Candlelit Dinner in the Restaurant.

MONDAY
8.00 - 10.00 am
English Breakfast and depart.

KNOW YOUR VOCABULARY

20 **Look at this restaurant bill and answer the following questions.**

```
20-01-96        The Akbar
  19:07
Table No4       Indian Cuisine


                6Cs
        COVER                .4.20
         2 SET MEAL A       .23.90
         1 LAMB PASAND       .5.95
         1 CHICKEN TIKKA     .5.25
         1 ROGAN JOSH        .4.90
         1 NAWABI CHICKEN    .5.50
         1 PESHWA NAN        .1.50
         2 PULAO RICE        .3.10
         1 KEEMA NAN         .1.50
         2 RICE              .2.70
         1 RESTAURANT DRINK  .7.80
         3 FROM SWEET ROOM   .7.50
         1 SWEET             .1.60
         1 COFFEE            .0.90
        SUBTOTAL            .76.30
             12%
        SERVICE CHARGE       .9.16

        TOTAL               .85.46
```

1 What date did these people have dinner ?
2 What was the number of their table ?
3 What time did they arrive at the restaurant ?
4 How many people were there in this group ?
5 What was the service charge ?
6 What was the cost of this meal before the service charge ?
7 If you received this bill would you give the waiter a tip ?

21 **Fill in the spaces in the sentences below using the list of words to help you. There may be more than one right answer.**

give / take / send / bring / show / fetch

1 Waitress - could you .... me the menu, please ?
2 Shall we .... a picnic with us when we go out at the weekend ?
3 If you come back in ten minutes we'll have some fresh tomatoes - I'm just off to .... them.
4 Could you .... the bill, please ?
5 May I .... you to your table, sir ?
6 Would you .... these groceries round to my flat, please ?

22 **Learn these words. Listen to your teacher and mark the main word stress(es).**

For example: tŏtal

1	potatoes	5	pudding	9	thirsty	13	chicken
2	tomatoes	6	steak	10	salad	14	toast
3	cauliflower	7	sandwich	11	menu	15	steamed
4	honey	8	hungry	12	cabbage		

5 Health and Lifestyles

Lead-in

1   What sort of things make you laugh ?
Do you know any jokes ? Can you tell your class a joke in English ?
Is it difficult to tell a joke in a foreign language ?
Do you think the jokes below are funny ?

> DOCTOR: You need glasses.
> MAN: But I'm already wearing glasses.
> DOCTOR: In that case, I need glasses.

> - Doctor, doctor, people are always ignoring me.
> - Next please!

What makes 'Doctor, Doctor' jokes internationally funny ?

2   Label the parts of the body. The words you need are listed for you.
If you need help ask your partner or your teacher, or use a dictionary.

head

head
stomach
foot
tooth
finger
leg
back
neck
toe
heart
hand
knee
arm
thumb
chest

Reading

3   **What are the things you do to look and feel good ? For example, do you go swimming every day ? Do you eat a lot of fresh fruit ? Write down some of the things you do.**

4   **Now read the text below.**

• HEALTH ADVICE •
from our own doctor
LOOK GOOD and FEEL GOOD!

You are what you eat. If you eat badly your body will find ways of letting you know sooner or later. Extra weight, spotty skin, poor teeth and heart disease can all point to the fact that you are not eating properly. Your life style also plays an important part in your general health and your body needs time to relax after a meal.

The following do's and don'ts should help you keep fit:

- Do get plenty of fresh air - that way you'll sleep better.
- Do make sure you eat plenty of fresh fruit and vegetables.
- Don't overcook vegetables - either steam them or use a small amount of water so that they keep their goodness.
- Don't eat too much fat, sugar and salt.
- Do try to take some exercise at least three times a week - especially if you sit at a desk all day.

REMEMBER: EAT TO LIVE - DON'T LIVE TO EAT!

Where do you think you might read this ? What is the writer trying to do ?

5   **Now work in a small group with three or four others. Write five questions on this text. (Make sure you know the answers to your questions !) Exchange your questions with another group and be ready to check their answers.**

Speaking

6 **Answer these questions about yourself. For each one put a tick (✓) under Yes or No.**

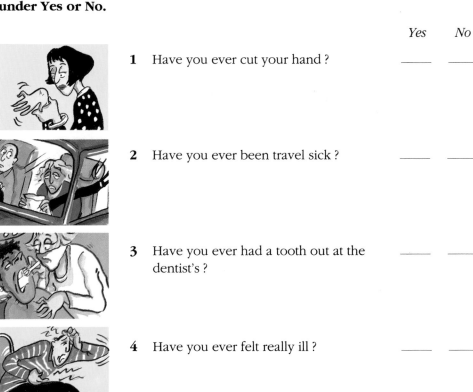

		Yes	*No*
1	Have you ever cut your hand ?	_____	_____
2	Have you ever been travel sick ?	_____	_____
3	Have you ever had a tooth out at the dentist's ?	_____	_____
4	Have you ever felt really ill ?	_____	_____

7 **Now be ready to put the same questions to people in your class. If the answer is 'Yes', find out more about what happened. For example:**

☐ How did you … ?
☐ When did you … ?
☐ Where were you … ?
☐ What did you do next ?
☐ What happened then ?

8 **Now write some questions to ask your partner using the following words to help you.**

  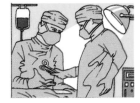  

1 burn / hand   **2** have / accident   **3** have / operation   **4** be / hospital   **5** eyes / tested

9 **Write down the answers to the questions you get from your partner. Check that what you and your partner have written is correct.**

Listening

10   Now listen to a patient at a doctor's surgery and fill in the details on the note which the doctor writes for the nurse. You will hear the piece twice.

TO: *Nurse Roberts*

FROM: *Dr Fisk*

PATIENT: *Mrs* 1 ....

accident at home

knocked over 2 ....

full of 3 ....

Severe burns on her 4 ....

I've taken off the bandage - can you please treat

Thanks

Listening

11   You are going to hear part of a radio programme called 'Lifestyles'. Two people, Maggie Brown and Rik Macey, talk about their different lifestyles. Before you listen, look at the statements below. Then as you listen, try to decide who said what: put M in the box if you think it was Maggie, R if you think it was Rik. One answer has been given for you.

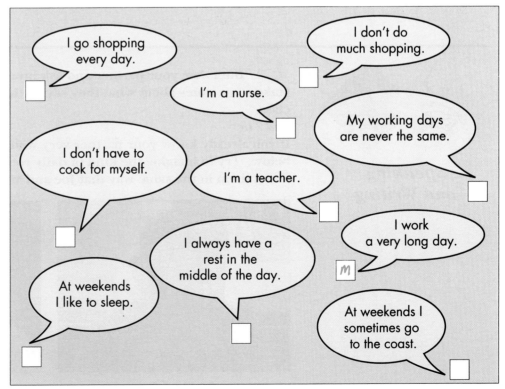

Reading

12 **Look at these two photographs. Try to guess where the people come from. What kind of families do you think they come from ?**
What sort of lives do you think they lead ?

13 **Now read how Joe and Maya spend their days.**

Daily routines

JOE

I get up at 6 every morning and help my dad. He has a flower shop so he has to be at the flower market by four. Then when he comes back we unload all the flowers into the shop. I usually take the telephone orders for him so he knows what he has to deliver that day. Then I make a cup of tea for my mum while she's still in bed, get my breakfast and go to school. At the weekend I work in the shop on Saturdays and help my mother arrange the flowers in the church for Sunday. Then on Sunday I go to church in the morning and the evening with my parents.

MAYA

I get up around midday because I'm usually at a party the night before and I never wake up in time for breakfast. Then I have a nice long bath, get dressed and call a friend to see who's free for lunch. I might go to my health club in the afternoon or do some shopping. And before I know where the day's gone it's time to get ready for another party. At the weekends I go to stay with some friends or maybe I pop over to Paris or even New York - just for a bit of fun! Or in the winter I might go ski-ing with my boyfriend. He's got his own chalet in Switzerland.

Speaking and Writing

14 **Interview your partner and ask how she/he spends her/his day. Make some notes about what they say so that you can tell the rest of the class.**
and / or
If you already know your partner very well, look at the photographs below. Try to imagine the kind of daily routine these people have. Write about them in the same way that Joe and Maya write about themselves.

Listening

15 You will hear different people talking. Look at the pictures and put a tick in the correct boxes.

In number 1 a person wants to make an appointment.
In number 2 a man is waiting for his prescription.
In number 3 a woman has taken her baby to a hospital emergency unit.
In number 4 a man is talking to his doctor.

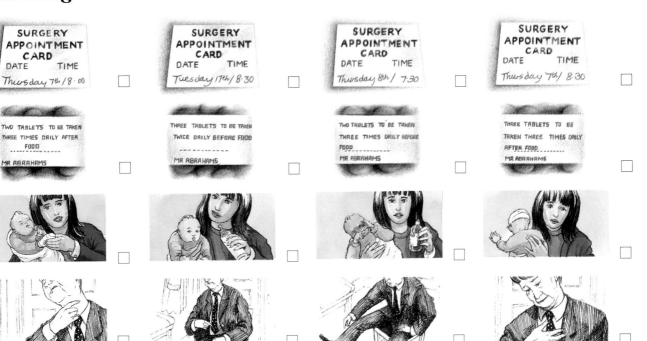

Speaking

16 Work with your partner on numbers 1-4. Take it in turns to be either A or B.

1   *A*   You want to make an appointment to see your dentist. You are in a lot of pain.
      B   You are the dentist's receptionist. The dentist is very busy.

2   *A*   You are in a chemist's. Explain to the chemist that you feel very sick and have a bad headache.
      B   Offer to sell the person some aspirin and suggest that they go home and lie down.

3   *A*   You have fallen off your bike and cut your leg very badly. A friend has brought you to the hospital emergency department.
      B   You ask the person's name and address and how the accident happened.

4   *A*   Tell the doctor that you think you have a fever and a pain in your chest.
      B   Be kind and sympathetic and tell the person that you think they have 'flu and should go to bed for a couple of days.

For Further Practice turn to page 124.

Grammar

▶ **VERB BASE + -ING AS NOUN**

17 **In some sentences a verb base + -ing can be a noun, and therefore the subject or object of a sentence. For example:**

Some people are afraid of going into hospital.

This can be written another way and still mean the same:

Going into hospital frightens some people.

18 Complete the following sentences.

1 Sitting at a desk all day ....
2 .... apples is good for your teeth.
3 Drinking alcohol ....
4 .... in poor light is bad for your eyes.

19 In the PET you may have to rewrite sentences like this in Part 1 of the Writing Paper of the test.
   Rewrite the following sentences.

1 Many people are frightened of growing old.
   Growing ....
2 It is bad for one's health to smoke.
   Smoking ....
3 It is very difficult for some people to lose weight.
   Losing ....
4 Some people are nervous of visiting the dentist.
   Visiting ....
5 It is bad for your heart to eat too much fatty food.
   Eating ....

▶ **VERBS ENDING WITH -ING AFTER CERTAIN VERBS AND PREPOSITIONS**

20 Examples:

nervous + of + -ing: I'm nervous of being alone at night.
afraid + of + -ing: I'm afraid of going in a lift.

Of course it is perfectly possible to use a noun instead of the -ing verb and say or write: 'I'm afraid of escalators' or 'I'm nervous of aeroplanes', *but* when a verb follows the preposition it must end with -ing.

21 Suggest ways of completing the following sentences using a suitable verb base + -ing

1 I apologise for …
2 I am interested in …
3 She was arrested for …

4 The man was prevented from …
5 They insisted on …

Reading

22   Read the text below. With your partner decide what the text is about. What is the connection between the text and the photograph ?

THE REACTIVART T-SHIRT

1990s GREEN FASHION

The 1990s may be the time ..... fashion designers show that they care about the environment. We now have New Age fashion which argues ..... clothes should be simple and use natural colours. This is supposed to fit in with all the green and natural way of thinking, ... how far are these clothes environmentally friendly?

Perhaps the only truly green fashion designers are from REACTIVART, a group of artists who create art from recycled material. Their recent fashion show in London offered clothes that really were environmentally friendly ...... they were made from already used materials.

Some people say that the new fashion shows a change of attitude ..... that one of the most important products of this change will be wool. Wool is a natural product, it's renewable and the sheep don't need to be killed for it.

It will be a matter of 'wait and see' before we discover ..... the latest fashion will really lead us back to nature.

23   A number of words have been missed out - what kind of words are missing ? Are they all the same kind of word ?

Your teacher will put a list of the missing words on the board but they will be in the wrong order. Read the text again and fill in the spaces using the list of words.

For Further Practice in reading turn to page 125.

Writing

24   You are studying in the UK. Each week you write a letter to your family. In this week's letter you are telling them about an accident you saw yesterday. Write about 80 words. An opening sentence has been written for you.

Anyway, I must tell you about something that happened yesterday.

....

KNOW YOUR VOCABULARY

25 **Can you match each picture with its correct text ?**

The five major world religions

A

B

C

4. Buddhism: a Buddist temple

2. Hinduism: an Indian temple

D

1. Judaism: prayers at the wailing wall in Jerusalem

5. Moslem: the Dome of the Rock in Jerusalem

3. Christianity: A British Parish church

E

26 **Name the following drawings using the list of words to help you.**

soap / toothbrush / toothpaste / comb / razor / hairbrush / scissors / drugs / to shave / clean laundry

27   A *chemist's* in the UK may also be called a *pharmacy* but in the USA it is called a *drugstore*.

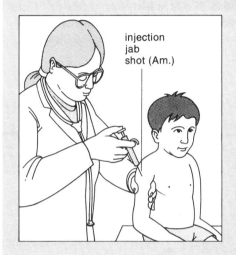
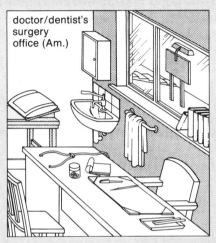
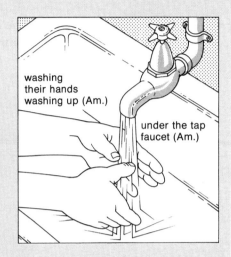

28   Learn these words. Listen to your teacher and mark the main word stresses.

For example: medicine

1	cough	**6**	blood
2	wound	**7**	ache
3	hygiene	**8**	specialist
4	dead	**9**	surgeon
5	die	**10**	death

29   What's up with you ?

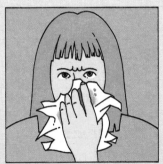

I've got a sore throat.   I've got a cold.   I've got earache.   I've got a nosebleed.

6 Holidays and Travel

Lead-in

1 How good is your world geography ? Work with your partner. Can you name the countries below ? Give yourselves one minute and choose your answers from the list.

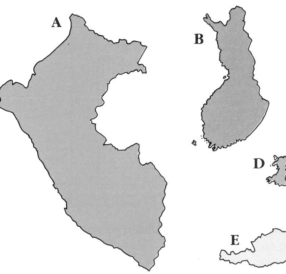

Austria
Egypt
Finland
Wales
The Czech
 Republic
Kenya
Sri Lanka
Canada
Peru
The Philippines

2 Now find the capital city of each country you have chosen: for example the capital city of Greece is Athens. Use the list below to help you.

Nairobi / Ottawa / Cardiff / Vienna / Lima / Helsinki / Cairo / Colombo / Manila / Prague

Listening

3 Look at this map. Some of the towns have been labelled for you. Can you name any of the others ? Use another map or ask your teacher to help you.

4 Now listen to Amy and Ted who are planning a touring holiday in the UK. As you listen, see if you can mark their route on your map.

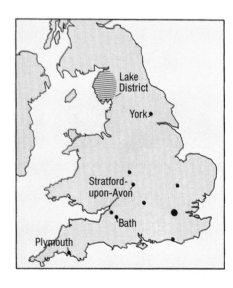

Reading

5   **Now look at this page of advertisements from an accommodation guide to the Lake District. Work with a partner and answer Yes or No to questions 1-5.**

GRASMERE HOTEL

Rooms: 4 single, 5 double
Shower/bath: in most rooms
Rates: bed and breakfast, single from £20 to £25, double from £30 to £35
Parking: 9 spaces

COUNTRY WAYS

Rooms: 1 single, 5 double/twin
Shower/bath: in all rooms
Rates: bed and breakfast, single from £29.95 to £37.35, double from £39.95 to £42.00
Parking: 10 spaces
Closed: 1 week Christmas

WASHINGTON HOTEL

Rooms: 16 single, 21 double/twin
Shower/bath: in most rooms
Rates: bed and breakfast, single from £21 to £32, double from £32 to £45
Parking: 20 spaces
Animals taken by prior arrangement
A warm welcome and high standard await you at the Washington. It offers good value for business people and tourists alike. All rooms have colour TV, radio, tea and coffee, hairdryer and telephone. The Washington Supper Room offers reasonably priced dinners from Monday to Thursday. The hotel's pleasant and convenient location makes it ideal for exploring.

REDWOOD LODGE

Rooms: 112 double/twin
Shower/bath: in all rooms
Rates: bed and breakfast, single from £60 to £75, double from £70 to £85
Parking: 1,000 spaces, coach parking
Redwood Lodge is a unique hotel and leisure centre. All bedrooms are furnished with colour TV/radio, tea/coffee-making facilities, trouser-presses and hairdryers. During their stay, hotel guests become members of Europe's largest country club which boasts squash, tennis, badminton, snooker, swimming pools, sauna, solarium, gymnasium, cinema, coffee shop and 4 bars.

ORCHARD HOUSE

Rooms: 1 single, 3 double/twin
Rates: bed and breakfast, single £11.75, double £23.50
Parking: 8 spaces

		Yes	No
1	Orchard House is the cheapest hotel.	——	——
2	The Washington Hotel has a bath or shower in all rooms.	——	——
3	Country Ways has more double than single rooms.	——	——
4	All the rooms in Redwood Lodge have a bathroom.	——	——
5	The Grasmere Hotel charges up to £40 a night for a double room.	——	——

6   **Amy and Ted want a small hotel, two single rooms (preferably with bath/shower), at not more than £22 a night each. Which hotel was their first choice ? Which hotel was their second choice ?**

For Further Practice in reading advertisements turn to page 126.

Writing

7 **Amy has to write a letter to book accommodation for herself and Ted. Look at the letter below and see if you can fill in the missing words.**

7 Ashley Villas,
Periton Place,
Bath BA2 6SR
Avon.

April 12th 1996

.... Sir / Madam
I .... like to book two ....
rooms .... 3 nights .... August 8th
to August 10th. If possible I would
like .... have rooms .... either a
bath .... a shower. Thank you.

Yours .... ,

Amy Northcott (Ms.)

For Further Practice in writing turn to page 126.

Reading

8 **Work with a partner. Read the four holiday postcards and answer the questions.**

1 Who is on holiday by the coast ?
2 Who has to walk downhill to go shopping ?
3 Who is finding life uncomfortable ?
4 Who is getting the most exercise ?

May 4th
Am staying in a small inn in
the mountains - you can just
see it in the photograph! The
view from my window is
fantastic - snow on the
mountain tops and a lake
nearby. Am getting plenty of
fresh air + exercise - the
nearest shop is 2 kms away
at the bottom of the valley!

See you soon, love, Olly

Gerry Greyson,
Sharpwick Cottage,
Inverkeilor,
nr. Arbroath,
Angus,
Scotland

A

Hi!   26/7
This is a great place. We're
walking miles in these
forests and never meet
anyone. Have taken lots
of photos - the plants
and flowers are
beautiful - some we've
never seen before.
Will ring you when
we get back. See you,
          H. & D.

Mrs E. Snelgrove,
14 Rookery Road
Retford,
Notts.
U.K.

B

15th August
The beaches round here are lovely. We've been swimming every morning although the sea is quite cold. In the afternoons we sunbathe or wander into the town which is full of interesting shops. Hope all's well, Katy

Yvonne Meadway,
16, Station Road,
READING,
Berks.

C

Sept. 2nd
We're camping beside this lake which is a nice spot to be if you like insects! They certainly like us. Otherwise everything's fine - plenty to do sailing, swimming and water-skiing. Beautiful scenery too. Hope to see you when we return,
J+J xxxx

Mr John Jacobs
9 The Dippons,
Shifnal,
SHROPSHIRE

D

9 **Now look at the four pictures on the postcards. Can you decide who sent which card ?**

1

2

3

4

10 **Look at the two pictures below. Choose one of these and write a postcard to a friend or someone in your family.**
Remember to say where you are and what you are doing.

Speaking

11 **Work with a partner. Look at the details for four different holidays. You and your partner have to decide where you would like to go for one week. (All the holidays start from the UK but you should work out the cost of your holiday in your own currency.)**
   Be ready to tell your teacher:

☐ where you have decided to go
☐ why you have chosen this holiday and how much it will cost
☐ what you expect to do
☐ the flight details
☐ the accommodation details

New York

Chatwal Manhattan

This newly refurbished hotel is on 48th Street close to Broadway, Times Square and convenient for museums and shops. The hotel has a restaurant, coffee lounge and cocktail lounge. The 400 modern rooms all have private bath or shower, colour TV, telephone and air conditioning.
NO ROOM CHARGE for up to 2 children under 12 sharing room with 2 adults.
ROOM ONLY
Single Room Supplement £27.00 per night.

BRITISH AIRWAYS
THE WORLD'S FAVOURITE AIRLINE

Holiday Ref. T85 CHATWAL MANHATTAN NYC01	LONDON					
		Wed	Dly			
		Thu	Thu	Exc	Dly	
	Fri	Fri	Fri	Sun	Exc	
Days of Departure	Sat	Sat	Sat	Mon	Sun	Dly
Number of Nights in Hotel	2	3	4	5	6	7
1 Jan-31 Mar	369	389	421	442	464	487
1 Apr-30 Jun	427	449	478	501	524	549
1 Jul-31 Aug	444	469	493	517	540	564
1 Sep-31 Oct	427	453	478	501	524	549
21 Nov-11 Dec & 25-31 Dec	389	418	441	464	488	512
12 Dec-24 Dec	488	513	535	557	578	601

SPAIN

ROSAS
HOSTAL SANT JORDI

Location: Simple but good quality two star hotel near the sandy beach and about half a mile from the centre of Rosas.
Various sports facilities are available locally: mini golf, windsurfing, sailing, horse-riding, cycling, pedalos, deep-sea diving and waterskiing. There is a golf course at Playa de Pals.

Facilities: The Hostal San Jordi is well-equipped and very suitable for family holidays. Facilities include: restaurant with buffet breakfast, bar (open all day), lounge, gaming machines, open-air swimming pool with children's pool, garden and sun terrace with bar service and children's playground. The hotel has its own car park.

Accommodation:
Type A: 2/3 person room with bath, shower and toilet.
Type B: 2/4 person room with bath, shower and toilet.
Type C: single room with bath, shower and toilet.

SANT JORDI
PRICES ARE IN £'s PER PERSON PER WEEK

FULL BOARD	A	B	C
29/4-26/5, 23/9-30/9	99	99	126
27/5-7/7	123	123	150
8/7-25/8	172	172	199
26/8-22/9	138	138	165

Arrival is on Saturday. Minimum stay: 7 nights.
Except from 29/4 to 1/7 when arrival is free on request and minimum stay is 7 nights.

ITALY

BARDOLINO
HOTEL IDANIA**

Location: Good two-star hotel in the centre of Bardolino, about 400 metres from Lake Garda. Everything you need for a successful holiday is to be found here. Watersports fanatics are close to the lake and for those who love bustle, the centre of the town is close by.

Facilities: Hotel Idania offers you a restaurant with breakfast buffet and a choice of 3-course menus, bar, pleasant lounges with TV corner, open-air swimming pool with sun terrace and bar service.
Dances are held several times a week and excursions are organised for the guests.

Accommodation:
Type A: two/three person room with shower, toilet and telephone.
Type B: single room with shower, toilet and telephone.

IDANIA
PRICES ARE IN £'s PER PERSON PER WEEK

HALF BOARD	A	B
18/3-2/6, 23/9-14/10	138	166
3/6-30/6, 2/9-22/9	164	192
1/7-1/9	206	234

Arrival is on Saturday.
Minimum stay: 7 nights.

Moscow

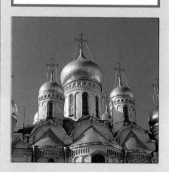

Prices in £s per person sharing a double/twin room

MOSCOW			
	DEPARTURES ON OR BETWEEN		
	1 Jan-25 Mar	26 Mar-31 Oct	1 Nov-31 Dec
NTS			
3	195	234	204
5	248	287	257

FLIGHT DETAILS				
DEPARTURE POINT	NTS	APPROXIMATE DEP.TIME RTN.TIME		HOLIDAY NUMBER
HEATHROW	3	Thu. 09.50	Sun. 18.45	LH3T
HEATHROW	3	Fri. 09.50	Mon. 18.45	LH3
HEATHROW	5	Thu. 09.50	Mon. 18.45	LH5

SUPPLEMENTS £'s PER PERSON PER NIGHT
• Single room £6.

Included in the Price

• Return tickets from Heathrow to Moscow.
• Return transfers between the airport and your hotel.
• Hotel accommodation with full board.

Grammar

▶ PASSIVE SENTENCES

12 **Look at these two sentences. Which one do you think sounds more natural in English ? Can you say why ?**

1 People grow cotton in Egypt.
2 Cotton is grown in Egypt.

The second sentence uses the present simple passive: is/are + past participle.

The passive is often used in newspaper reports and in sentences where the person who does something, or the cause of something, is less important. For example:

3 A new car was stolen from a garage yesterday.

instead of:

4 Someone stole a new car from a garage yesterday.

Sentence 3 uses the past simple passive: was/were + past participle.

Notice that if we do want to say who is responsible in a passive sentence we use by.

In the PET you may have to change sentences in Question 6 from active to passive or passive to active, like examples 1-4 above.

If the original tense is progressive, for example:

5 The police are looking into the causes of the rail crash.

then the passive sentence will be:

6 The causes of the rail crash are being looked into by the police.

- is/are (present tense) + being + past participle.

Similarly, in the past tense:

7 They were still building the hotel when I arrived for my holiday.
8 My hotel was still being built when I arrived for my holiday.

- was/were (past tense) + being + past participle.

13 **Rewrite the following sentences. Make sure you keep the original tense the same.**

1 The flight was booked by my friend.
   My friend ....

2 They make cars in the USA.
   Cars ....

3 The customs officer stopped the man as he got off the plane.
   The man ....

4 We are drinking more coffee than ever nowadays.
   Coffee ....

5 Someone brought tea into England in the seventeenth century.
   Tea ....

6 Scientists are making new discoveries all the time.
   New discoveries ....

7 Someone broke into the bank yesterday.
The bank ....

8 A heavy snowfall delayed the train.
The train ....

9 People sell many different things in the market.
Many different things ....

10 A new Hong Kong airport is being planned for next century.
The government ....

▶ **WHICH / THAT / WHO / WHOM / WHOSE**

14 **Use the following words to fill in the gaps in the sentences below. In some cases no word may be necessary, in others it may be possible to use more than one word.**

which / that / who / whom / whose

1 Brazil produces the best coffee .... you can buy.

2 The hotel .... burnt down was built two hundred years ago.

3 .... are you going on holiday with?

4 Do you know .... luggage this is?

5 The foreign students .... I teach are very friendly.

6 The Greek island .... is the most popular is also the most expensive.

15 **Look at the different texts below. Listen to the various people talking and fill in the missing information. You will need to write one word, a short phrase or some numbers. You will hear everything twice.**

Listening

the rail travellers' guide to biking by train

BIKING

2 Welcome to
~ CENTURY HOTEL ~
Name ....
Date .... to ....
Type of room ....
Price per night ....
Booked in by ..*nLG*.........................
Room No.

% 33 That's what students can save on travel costs STUDENT COACHCARD

4 Train Times
Liverpool → Leeds
dep: ....
Leeds → Liverpool
dep: ....
Remember label !!

Student Coach Card
Get ....
and a letter from
....
Costs
Office will do it over
the counter

5

ROOM MAINTENANCE

Will you please assist us to keep our rooms in better condition.

If anything in this room needs the attention of our Engineering or Housekeeping Departments please complete this form.

ROOM NO. ....
DATE .... TIME ....
....
....
PLEASE LEAVE AT FRONT DESK FOR PROMPT ACTION
Thank you for your time

1

SCHWEIZERHOF BERN
With compliments Date: ....
Weather forecast
☀ ☁ ☁ ☂ ❄
Outside temperature
.... °C .... °F

3

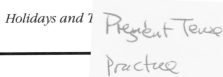

Reading

16   What is your favourite form of travel ? Bike, ca
For short distances perhaps you prefer to go on foot.
travel a long distance, however, would you go by plan
by bus or coach, or by train ?

The text below is about travelling throughout Europe by train. Your friend has given you a list of questions about Inter-Rail. Read the information and then answer Yes or No to questions 1-8. (One has been answered for you.)

INTER RAIL
FOR UNDER 26's

The Inter-Rail card allows free travel on the rail networks of most European countries, plus Morocco. You can use it to travel around Austria, Belgium, Denmark, Finland, France, Germany, Greece, Hungary, Republic of Ireland, Italy, Luxembourg, Morocco, the Netherlands, Norway, Portugal, Rumania, Spain, Sweden, Switzerland, Turkey (European lines only) and Yugoslavia. And there are reduced price tickets for travel in Great Britain and Northern Ireland as well as for Hoverspeed hovercraft, most Sealink ships and other ferry services.

You're free to go as you please - you'll find that rail is a great way to discover the countries you travel through. Make a tour of Europe's cities and cultural centres, or just find somewhere you like and use local trains to explore the region.

Your Inter-Rail card is valid for one month from the date you choose. If you want to spend more than a month travelling then all you have to do is buy two or more cards.

BUYING INTER-RAIL
To buy an Inter-Rail card, you must be under 26 on the first day of the card's validity. You can buy Inter-Rail in Great Britain and Northern Ireland, provided that you can prove that you have been a resident of this country for at least six months immediately prior to purchase.

CONTINENTAL TRAINS
It's often a good idea to reserve seats or sleeping berths, especially for busy periods, long journeys and travel by hovercraft or Jetfoil. Details and reservations can be obtained from principal BR Travel Centres or appointed travel agents. Your Inter-Rail card does not guarantee sleeping or seating accommodation.

There are two main types of sleeping accommodation on European railways.

Couchettes look like ordinary compartments but at night they are converted to sleep up to six people - rugs and pillows are provided. They are quite cheap and should preferably be reserved in advance.

Sleeping car berths are more expensive. They usually have two or three berths in each compartment plus a wash basin, and are converted into private compartments for daytime travel.

WHERE TO STAY
The YMCA offers budget priced accommodation and informal hospitality during July, August and September, to Inter-Rail travellers of both sexes at YMCA Inter-Points throughout Europe.

1   Is there an age limit on Inter-Rail ?
2   Can I use the Inter-Rail card on ferry crossings ?
3   Does it last for more than one month ?
4   Do I have to be British to get one ?
5   Do I need a passport when I apply for one ? *No*
6   Do I have to book seats in advance ?
7   Is a couchette expensive ?
8   Is there any information about accommodation abroad?

For Further Practice in reading turn to page 127.

Writing

17 The Fact Sheet below is incomplete. Your teacher will ask you to complete it for homework. You can look up information in a library or ask your friends or colleagues for help. The last line is for your own country, but if your country is already on the list you must choose another ! When you have finished you can compare your information with your partner's.

COUNTRY (language)	POPULATION	CAPITAL	CURRENCY	CLIMATE
UNITED KINGDOM English	57,750,000	London	sterling	cool, rainy, fog in winter
SPAIN	39,322,000	Madrid	....	sunny in the south but cold in the north
.... Italian	57,747,000	....	lira	cold winters in the north, hot and dry in summer
BELGIUM 1) .... 2)	10,022,000	....	....	cool and wet
JAPAN	....	....	....	
TURKEY	....	....	....	
....	....	....	....	

KNOW YOUR VOCABULARY

18 Listen to your teacher and mark the main word stress for the months of the year.

January	March	May	July	September	November
February	April	June	August	October	December

19 Learn the seasons of the year and practise saying them.

Spring / Summer / Autumn (Am. Eng. Fall) / Winter

20 Learn these words. Listen to your teacher and mark the main word stress.

For example: geography

1	scenery	**4**	thunder	**7**	terminal	**10**	earth
2	zero	**5**	lightning	**8**	immigration	**11**	stewardess
3	temperature	**6**	shade	**9**	frontier	**12**	harbour

21 Use this list of words to label these pictures.

platform	carriage	check-in desk	boarding card	road sign
moon	star	lorry	caravan	canal

7 Education

1 **Look at the photographs of the eight people. Find out who is who.**

Lead-in

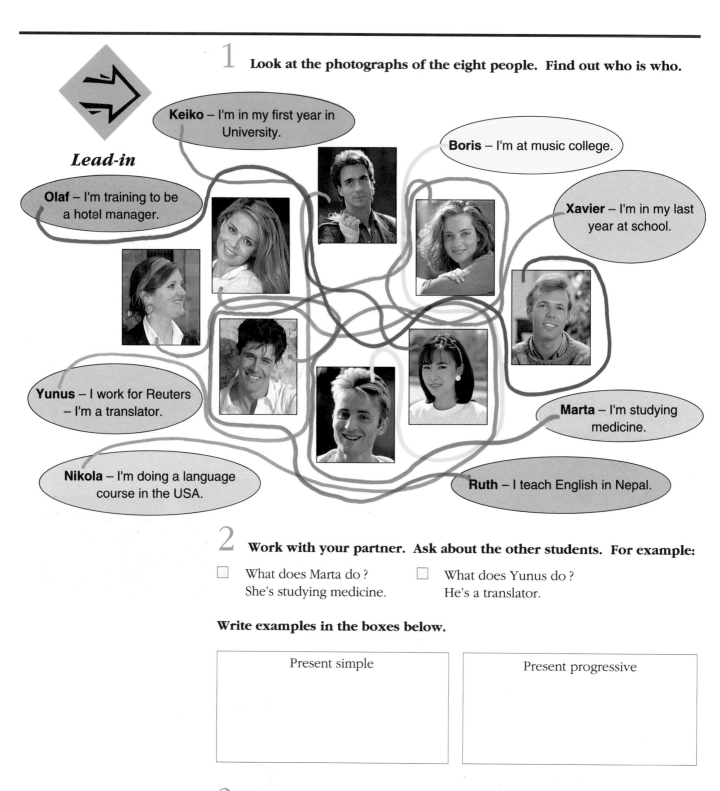

Keiko – I'm in my first year in University.

Boris – I'm at music college.

Olaf – I'm training to be a hotel manager.

Xavier – I'm in my last year at school.

Yunus – I work for Reuters – I'm a translator.

Marta – I'm studying medicine.

Nikola – I'm doing a language course in the USA.

Ruth – I teach English in Nepal.

2 **Work with your partner. Ask about the other students. For example:**

☐ What does Marta do ?
She's studying medicine.

☐ What does Yunus do ?
He's a translator.

Write examples in the boxes below.

Present simple	Present progressive

3 **What about you ? Are you a student ? Do you go to school/college/university ? Or do you go out to work ?**
Be ready to tell your teacher what you do.

Reading

4 **Look at the article below. Where do you think you would read a text like this ? What can you tell from the photograph about the life the children lead ? What can you see behind the children ?**
  Look back at the map in Unit 6 (page 52) and find Oxford. Oxfordshire is one of the counties next to Gloucestershire, which you read about in Unit 1.

Sarah Lonsdale visits some travelling families in Oxfordshire

Wandering Free

Their father chops up firewood for fire to cook breakfast over, they sleep out in the woods and they haven't been to school for years.

They are travellers' children, living in vans and buses. Their parents make a living by doing different jobs like collecting and selling old pieces of metal.

These parents have chosen not to send their children to school, and anyway very often the schools don't want to have the children.

Some of the counties near London are particularly popular areas for travellers. They can make good money doing odd jobs, there is plenty of commonland where they can park their vehicles and the countryside is beautiful. Oxfordshire is especially popular because the authorities there provide a school bus which once a week brings a 'classroom' to the travellers.

Nine-year-old Anna has not been to school for two years. She has a very free life running around the woods, playing with animals, and never has any homework. However, she can read as well as any other nine-year-old, says the teacher, who

Lizzie, Anna and Sofia: Anna says "We hate school because of all the rules. But I like the school bus, it's fun."

drives the bus around the county, visiting a different travellers' camp each day.

Anna's mother has taught her to read and write and Anna reads stories to the younger children.

During the weekly lessons in the school bus Anna and her friends read, draw and paint.

The children love their lifestyle and hate the idea of returning to school. 'I never want to go to school again,' said Anna, 'but I wouldn't mind coming to the bus every day, it's fun.'

---

5 **Read the passage and answer the questions by choosing the best answer A, B, C or D.**

1 The children's parents

  A are out of work.
  B have no money.
  C do various jobs.
  D live in a big hut.

2 The children

  A love going to school.
  B hate travelling around.
  C dislike meeting people.
  D enjoy their lifestyle.

For Further Practice in reading turn to page 128.

Grammar

▶ **PREPOSITIONS 1**

6 **Fill in the gaps in the sentences using prepositions from the list below.**

with / for / in

1 What is this called .... Portuguese ?
2 What is the Dutch word .... 'school' ?
3 How do you say 'goodbye' .... Russian ?
4 My language course starts .... two weeks' time.
5 I'm going to have private lessons .... my English teacher.
6 Can you translate this letter .... me please - I don't speak Danish.

▶ **PREPOSITIONS 2**

7 **Use the prepositions below to fill in the gaps.**

to / on / during / at / in

Milos lives .... home with his parents. He studies History ....
university and goes .... classes every weekday except Wednesday.
.... Wednesdays he works .... a restaurant to earn some money.
He starts work .... eleven in the morning and finishes ....
midnight. .... this time he helps in the kitchen and serves in the restaurant.

▶ **PREPOSITIONS 3**

8 **Read the sentences below and put a line under each preposition. (There are eleven altogether.) For each sentence put a tick under the correct picture.**

1 Milos walks across the park to the university.
2 He walks along the path by the lake.
3 The university is near the park.
4 He walks down the steps.
5 Then he goes into the building.
6 He walks up to the second floor to the library.
7 He takes a book off the shelf and sits down to read.

1

2

4

6

3

5

7

▶   **MUST + INFINITIVE WITHOUT TO**

9   **We use** must **when we want to express obligation and this obligation comes from the speaker. For example:**

1   You must have a passport if you want to travel.
2   If you want to borrow books from the library you must have a ticket.

Can you think of an example from your own country using must **? For example, 'In Morocco you must drive on the right.'**

▶   **MUSTN'T (MUST NOT) + INFINITIVE WITHOUT TO**

10   **We use** mustn't **when we want to express the obligation** *not* **to do something because it is forbidden. For example:**

1   You mustn't smoke inside the hospital.
2   You mustn't park your car in the middle of a road.

Can you think of an example from your own country using mustn't **? For example, 'In the UK you mustn't dial 999 unless it's an emergency.'**

▶   **OUGHT TO AND SHOULD**

11   Ought to **and** should **are both used to give advice and are interchangeable. For example:**

1a   You ought to wear a coat when the weather's cold.
 b   You should wear a coat when the weather's cold.
2a   You oughtn't to be so noisy when people are trying to sleep.
 b   You shouldn't be so noisy when people are trying to sleep.

▶   **HAVE TO**

12   **We can also use** have to **to express a sense of obligation, but then the idea of obligation usually comes from an external rule or law. For example:**

1   You have to fill in an application form if you want to go to university.
2   In the UK you have to be eighteen before you can vote.

Can you think of an example using have to **based on your own country's rules ?**

If we want to make this verb negative or use it in a question form we add 'don't/didn't' depending on whether it is present or past. For example:

3   You don't have to be eighteen to get married in the UK, do you ?
4   Before 1989 you didn't have to pay to have your eyes tested in the UK.

REMEMBER

1 In some cases more than one answer will be possible. Obviously *must, should* and *ought to* can be interchangeable in the way that they can all be used to express advice. You will need to think about the kind of advice being given. A parent giving advice to a child will probably say 'It's very cold today so you must wear your coat', but a secretary to a boss will probably say 'You ought to think about wearing your coat as it's very cold today'.

2 You also need to think about whether the expression of obligation is personal or comes from a rule or law when deciding to use *must* or *have to*.

13 Complete the following sentences using:

must / mustn't   should / shouldn't
ought to / oughtn't to   have to / don't have to

1 You .... drive on the left in the UK.
2 If you feel tired you .... go to bed.
3 You .... work hard if you want to pass your exams.
4 If you have heart trouble you .... smoke.
5 If you want to go climbing you .... buy some boots.
6 In some countries you .... pay extra for school textbooks.
7 You .... borrow people's things without asking them first
8 If you want to go on a sailing holiday you .... learn to swim.
9 All travellers to China .... have a visa.
10 You .... pay to join a library in the UK as it's free.

Speaking and Writing

14 Anna and her friends like reading, drawing and painting. *The Early Times* asked 500 students in the UK their opinions about school. Mathematics and geography were the least favourite school subjects. Craft, design and technology were the favourite subjects.

The diagrams below show you the differences in the girls' and boys' answers. For example: More boys than girls like music, but games is more popular with girls than boys.

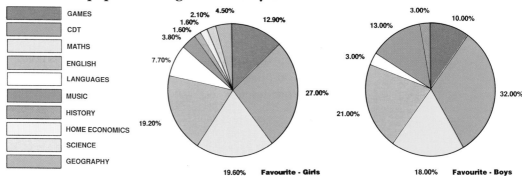

GAMES
CDT
MATHS
ENGLISH
LANGUAGES
MUSIC
HISTORY
HOME ECONOMICS
SCIENCE
GEOGRAPHY

Favourite - Girls   **Favourite - Boys**

1 What is/was your favourite subject ?
2 What is/was your least favourite subject ?
3 If you have left school do you think things have changed ? For example, are new or different subjects now being taught ?
4 Is/was there a subject which you want/wanted to do but is/was not available because of your sex ?
5 Do you think certain subjects are really only suitable for the male or female sex ?
6 Do you think you should be able to choose which subjects you do, or should some subjects always be compulsory ?

Interview as many people as you can and ask them questions 1 and 2. Use the information to draw two diagrams - one for each sex.

15 Now write a short report using the information from your diagrams. Are the answers similar to the answers given by students in the UK ?

Listening

16 Look at this advertisement.

Somerset Study Programmes

- Intensive programmes for people who need English
- Maximum of 8 students per class
- Full or part time
- Accommodation arranged
- Friendly atmosphere
- Prices on request Tel: 0497 18977

Mr Yacoub wants to send his daughter on an English language course. He has read the SSP advertisement and decides to ring their office. These are the questions he wants to ask.

SSP

1. Intensive programme? ....

....

....

+ speakers on 2 evenings a week

2. Check on class size ....

3. Full time? 6 hours a day
    Part time? ....

4. Accommodation? ....
                          or ....

5. Cost? - will send details

Listen to the telephone conversation and fill in the answers to his questions.

Writing

17 Look at the advertisement below. Part of it has been torn. Work with your partner and decide what the words should be.

THE

UNIVERSITY

MEETING INTERESTING PEOPLE

1 or 2 week programme
Choice of activities including:

photography
music
tennis an

Cost includes all meals
accommoda
drinks
tran
enter

18 You would like to know more about this Summer University. With your partner write down five questions you would ask.

19 Now write a letter to the Director for more information. The letter has been started for you. Write about 80 words.

The Director,
Summer University
MALTON   April 9 199......

Dear Sir / Madam,
I have seen an advertisement for the Summer University in
Malton and I would like to have some more information
about it. ....

Reading

20 Work with a partner. Look at the information on the opposite page. Match each of texts A - E with a sign or a notice 1 - 5.
When you have matched them, choose one heading from the list below for each of the texts. (Three headings will be left over.)

school handbook
dictionary
student accommodation
government information

politics
college timetable
library services
worldwide organisation

A OTHERS PROMISE THE MOON. ONLY THE GREEN PARTY GUARANTEES THE EARTH.

VOTE GREEN PARTY

TEN GOOD REASONS TO VOTE GREEN

1 RENEWAL OF BOOKS
Books may usually be renewed if not in demand. You may bring them to the library for renewal or have this done by post or telephone. When renewing by post or telephone the number shown below the bar code must be quoted (see example below) as well as the number on your membership card.

Book No **1021556**

B Join a Group
If you want to take a more active part in Amnesty's work then join one of the British Section's 294 groups.

3 AMNESTY INTERNATIONAL

REDBRICK POLYTECHNIC **4**

5 MEMBERSHIP➤ I/We wish to apply for membership of The Green Party

NAME(S) ....

....

ADDRESS ....

....

POSTCODE .... © ....

SIGNATURES ....

....

E Students resident in the city are not offered accommodation at the start of session except in very exceptional circumstances.

2 What is Social Security?

D If you're about to leave school or have just left, whether you're looking for a job, or doing a full-time course at college or university, or doing vacation work, this leaflet is for you. It tells you about the Social Security benefits you may be able to get.

C SOMERSET COUNTY LIBRARY

WELLS LIBRARY
The Library,
Union Street,
Wells,
BA5 2PU.
Telephone: 72292

HOURS OF OPENING
Monday	10.00-6.00
Tuesday	10.00-6.00
Thursday	10.00-6.00
Friday	10.00-7.30
Saturday	9.30-4.00

Writing

21   Now look at the newspaper headlines 1 and 2. Imagine these headlines are from an English language newspaper *in your own country*. Write the opening sentence(s) which might appear under these headlines.

Busy weekend of voting

1

Election results mean change at the top

2

Speaking

22 **Work with a partner and ask each other the following questions.**

☐ Do you remember your first day at school ?
☐ What can you remember about it ?
☐ What did you like most ? What did you like least ?
☐ Was there a particular teacher you liked ?

23 **Now look at this photograph. Discuss the following points with each other and be ready to talk to your teacher and the rest of the class.**

☐ Where are these children ?
☐ How old are they ?
☐ What are they doing ?
☐ Do they look interested ?
☐ Was this your experience ?

For Further Practice in speaking turn to the photograph on page 129.

Listening

24 **Work with your partner. If you don't understand something in a foreign language, what are the ways you can ask for help ? Write down a list of your suggestions.**

25 **Now you will hear various short conversations. Different people are asking for help in understanding things. The pictures below show you where the different speakers are.**

You must write down what they say when they ask for help. You will hear each conversation twice. Try to write down their exact words.

KNOW YOUR VOCABULARY

26 **Use these words to label the pictures below.**

pupil / queen / president / king / student / old-aged pensioner / lecturer

27 **Match these words with their definitions.**

war / peace / prime minister / state / politics

When a country has ▇▇ or is at ▇▇ it is not involved in a war.

A ▇▇▇ is the leader of the government of a country.

A ▇▇▇ is a period of fighting between countries or states when weapons are used and lots of people get killed.

1 ▇▇▇ refers to the actions or activities which people use to achieve power in a country, society, or organization or which ensure that power is used in a particular way.
2 Someone's ▇▇▇ are their beliefs about how a country ought to be governed.

6 A ▇▇ is **6.1** a country, usually when it is considered in terms of its political organization and structure. ... **6.2** one of the areas or divisions in a country such as the USA or Australia.

28 **Learn these words. Listen to your teacher and mark the main word stress(es).**

For example: mathematics

1	examination	**5**	conservative	**9**	professor	**13**	term (Am.Eng.
2	government	**6**	primary	**10**	translate		semester)
3	socialist	**7**	secondary	**11**	fail	**14**	pronounce
4	communist	**8**	professional	**12**	pass	**15**	certificate

8 Entertainment

Lead-in

1 Look at this face.
Does it look happy or sad ? Now turn your book upside down. Has the face changed ?

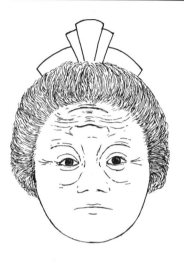

2 Work with a partner. Look at these photographs of famous people.

A

B

C

D

E

F

How many of them do you recognise ? Can you put names to them all ?
What are they famous for ? How famous are they in your country ?
Ask your partner: If you could choose to meet a famous person who would it be ? Why ?

3 What nationality are the people in these photographs ?
Now think of a famous person from your country. Who have you chosen and why is she/he famous ? Be ready to tell your teacher.

Reading

4 'Early Times' is an independent newspaper for young people which is published weekly. Many of the articles are written by young people themselves.

Below are the questions which one young reader put to a DJ who works for Capital Radio. Read the four questions.

A capital job!

Zak interviewing Capital Radio DJ Pat Sharp

1 What jobs did you have before joining Capital Radio?

2 What advice do you have for anyone hoping to become a DJ?

3 How did you get into radio?

4 Do you think you will ever leave radio to concentrate on TV?

Which question do you think Zak put first ? What was his last question ? Now look at the DJ's replies.

A I used to do mobile discos for parties and weddings. I used to send off demo tapes to radio stations but I didn't get anywhere. Then I got a manager who helped me to the front of the queue.

B I worked on Radio One first and some local radio like Radio Mercury. I have also been on Sky TV for some time in Europe.

C Do hospital radio and discos, and get used to performing before lots of people.

D No, because I like radio better because it's just you and the listeners and with TV there's the producer, director, cameraman etc. and when you do radio you do it all yourself.

Can you match Zak's questions with the DJ's answers ?

Speaking

5 **Ask your partner about her/his favourite:**

☐ TV programme
☐ pop singer/group
☐ magazine
☐ video

Write down the replies and be ready to tell your teacher.

Reading

6 **Read the advertising information for various events in London. Each advertisement is offering something different.**

A

MOMI
MUSEUM
of the moving image
bfi on the South Bank

LIGHTS
CAMERA
ACT

B

NATIONAL
ARMY
MUSEUM
CHELSEA

THE SOLDIER'S
STORY

museum of LONDON

THE RICHES OF
ondon past

F

MUSIC
ON A
SUMMER
EVENING
1995
Kenwood
Marble Hill
Audley End
Wrest Park

ART95
The London Contemporary Art Fair
18 - 22 January 1995

The Business Design Centre
52 Upper Street Islington London N1 0QH

G

D

Bedside Mann...

Rock 'n' Roll

Cool Crook

Hot Jazz

Mannerisms!

Doo-Wop Dance Band

Funded by Camden

LONDON BOROUGHS GRANTS SCHEME

British Gas

Tues. 26th; Wed. 27th & Thurs. 28th December 5:30 pm

Fri. 29th December 5pm - Sat 30th December 12 noon

...oongate ⊖   * !FREE! *   ⊖ Barbican.

Barbican Centre

E

NT

ROYAL NATIONAL THEATRE

THE BIRMINGHAM ROYAL BALLET

7-11 FEBRUARY
AT 7.30 PM

8 & 11 FEBRUARY
AT 2.30 PM

SADLER'S WELLS
Sadler's Wells Theatre

BOX OFFICE: 0171 713 6000

I

THE NATIONAL GALLERY

Information & EVENTS 1995

H

Using the information in the advertisements complete the blue and yellow columns in the table below.

PLACE	WHAT IT'S ABOUT	EXTRACT NO.
LONDON MUSEUM	about the people who have lived in London	. . . .
BARBICAN CENTRE	. . . .	. . . .
. . . .	plays	. . . .
. . . .	dance	. . . .
KENWOOD	. . . .	. . . .
BUSINESS DESIGN CENTRE	. . . .	. . . . 2 . . . .
. . . .	the history of soldiers	. . . .
. . . .	art	. . . .
MOMI	. . . .	. . . .

7   Now look at the following extracts of information about the places in exercise 6.

   Match each piece of information and its advertisement by writing in the correct number in the pink column in the table above. (Don't worry if you don't understand everything.)

NATIONAL ARMY MUSEUM
CHELSEA

Royal Hospital Road, Chelsea, London SW3 4HT
Tel 0171-730 0717
Opening Hours
Daily 10.00am to 5.30pm
except 1 January, 24-26 December, Good Friday,
Early May Public Holiday.

Business Design Centre
52 Upper Street
Islington Green
London N1 0QH

Opening times:
18th - 20th Jan 11 - 8pm
21st - 22nd Jan 11 - 6pm

1   2

3

GETTING TO AND FROM THE CENTRE

On Foot
The Barbican Centre is signposted throughout the City of London. On the walkways in the Barbican area, follow the yellow line.

⊖ By Underground
Moorgate
Barbican open Sundays/Public holidays
8am-11.50pm
St Paul's
Bank
Liverpool Street

5

THEATRE INFORMATION

BOX OFFICE 0171-278 8916
Sadler's Wells Theatre, Rosebery Avenue, London EC1R 4TN. For reservations, information and telephone bookings call 0171-278 8916 (5 lines). Box Office open from 10.30am to 7.30pm Monday to Saturday, or until 6.30pm when no evening performance. Recorded information 0171-278 5450 (24 hours) Information Hotline 0171-278 0855

FIRST CALL
For instantly confirmed credit card bookings ring our principal ticket agency, First Call, on 0171-240 7200. Open 24 hours a day, 7 days a week. With Booking Fee.

ALL MAJOR CREDIT CARDS ACCEPTED
TICKET PRICES (including VAT)
Stalls £16, £13, £10
Dress Circle £16, £13
Upper Circle £9, £6, £4

4

HOW TO GET HERE
Kenwood Lakeside, Hampstead Lane
London NW3
Underground to Golders Green or Archway stations, then 210 bus to Kenwood
Bus 271 to Highgate Village, then 15 minutes walk
Green Line 734
Limited free car parking available.
Refreshments & Licenced Bar.

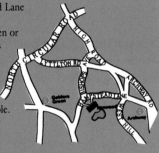

KENWOOD LAKESIDE CONCERTS	
ORDINARY CONCERTS	Adult
NUMBERED DECKCHAIRS	£5.00
SITTING ON THE GRASS	£3.50

6

FOYERS OPEN ALL DAY

Foyer open 10am - 11pm Mon-Sat

Food and Drink
Ovations The National's restaurant and wine bar. Open for lunch and dinner. Last orders 2pm or 11pm Reservations 0171 928 3531, 0171 928 2033 ext 561/ext 314 (Groups)
Lyttelton Terrace Café
Open 12 noon - 8pm.
Unreserved tables
Box Office Buffet
Open 10am - 11pm
Lyttelton Long Bar
Open 12 noon - 11pm
Other bars and buffets open prior to performance

Bookshops
One of London's leading theatre specialist bookshops.
Open 10am - 11pm (not Sunday)
10am - 8pm (Lyttelton non-performance days)
Enquiries:
0171 928 2033 ext 600

Backstage Tours
Daily (not Sunday).
£3.50 per person.
For groups of 12+, Students, Senior Citizens, Equity & BETA: £2.50.
Book on 0171 633 0880 or at the Lyttelton Information Desk.

Travel and Parking
Buses
1, 4, 68, X68, 168, 171, 171A, 176, 188, 501, 502, 513 to Waterloo Bridge; 70, 70A, 76 to Stamford St close by
Underground
Waterloo (Northern & Bakerloo lines)
Embankment (Circle & District lines) walk over Hungerford Bridge to South Bank Centre

7

INFORMATION

Museum of London
London Wall,
London EC2Y 5HN
Telephone 0171-600 3699

Museum opening times
Tuesday to Saturday
10.00am to 6.00pm (last admission 5.30pm)
Sunday 12 noon to 6pm (last admission 5.30pm)
Closed every Monday except bank holidays

How to find us
The Museum is situated at the junction of London Wall, Aldersgate Street and St Martin's-Le-Grand. The main entrance is located on the pedestrian highwalk. Nearest tube stations: Barbican, St Paul's, Moorgate, Bank. Buses: Museum of London 4, 141, 279a, 502; St Paul's 6, 8, 9, 9a, 11, 15, 22, 25, 501, 513.

8

bfi on the South Bank

• LOCATION •
SOUTH BANK CENTRE
WATERLOO, LONDON SE1 8XT
MOMI is situated right under Waterloo Bridge, behind the National Film Theatre, on London's South Bank

• OPENING HOURS •
10.00am - 6.00pm daily
(except 24-26 Dec)

9

The National Gallery
Trafalgar Square London
WC2N 5DN
Telephone 0171-839 3321

Recorded Information
0171-839 3526

Admission free

Gallery Hours: 10.00am-6.00pm Monday-Saturday.
2.00pm-6.00pm Sundays.
Closed New Year's Day, Good Friday, May Day Bank Holiday, Christmas Eve, Christmas Day and Boxing Day

Security Checks: For security purposes it may be necessary to check visitors' bags. Large items of luggage such as rucksacks, suitcases and musical instruments may not be deposited at the Gallery.

Listening

8 **Look back at the advertisements in exercise 6 and the table which you filled in. What would you like to visit if you were in London ?**

Listen to some people discussing what they are going to see or do in London. You will hear each conversation twice. Using the table in exercise 6 to help you, write down where they decide to go.

1   They decide to go ....
2   They are going to ....
3   They intend going to ....
4   They're off to ....
5   They've got tickets for ....

For Further Practice in listening turn to page 130.

Grammar

▶   **PHRASAL VERBS**

9 **A phrasal verb is a verb + a particle. (The particle may also be a preposition.) If you put a particle (sometimes even two particles) after the verb, this often changes the meaning of the verb. For example:**

1   If we run, we'll get to the theatre in time for the start of the play.

2   The child was run down and later died in hospital.

run + down: This means that the child was knocked over by a vehicle of some kind.

Here is a list of the most common verbs which are used to form phrasal verbs at the PET level.

take / look / go / get / put / turn

10 **Now look at the sentences below. In each case the verb is missing, although the particle is included. Fill in the missing verbs, but remember to put the verb into its correct form (e.g. simple past, present progressive etc.). Then underline the verb and its particle.**

Examples: How are you ...*getting*... on with your new flatmate ?
                      Can you ....*turn*...... down the radio please, it's terribly loud.

1   The local supermarket has .... up the prices again this week.
2   Could you .... after my baby for me while I go to the dentist ?
3   The gun .... off in his hands while he was cleaning it.
4   I like the colour of your T-shirt; it .... very well with your skirt.
5   I keep hearing loud screams - what's .... on next door ?

6   If you don't know a word, ... it up in a dictionary.
7   What time does your plane .... off ?
8   .... off the lights before you go to bed, please.
9   The policeman .... down the details of the accident.
10   The meeting .... on for much longer than anyone had expected.
11   'I'm .... you through now - hold the line please,' said the telephone operator.
12   When did you first .... up tennis ?
13   The lights .... off just as they sat down to eat.
14   .... out or you'll have an accident if you drive so carelessly !
15   José is .... along with his landlady and her family really well.
16   Once the fire had .... out the room became very cold.
17   We've .... off the meeting until next week when everyone will be back from holiday.
18   Do you know the story of the ugly duckling who .... into a beautiful swan ?
19   If you .... 177 away from 400 what are you left with ?
20   It's time for the news - let's .... on the TV.

► **IMPERATIVE VERBS**

11 **The imperative verb is used for giving orders.**

Feed your snake once a day

Keep off the grass

Turn left for the Camel House

12 **Fill in the following with a suitable imperative verb.**

1   Please .... the door.

2   Please don't .... food into the bear pit.

3   .... here for tickets to the zoo.

4   Don't .... the animals - they have a special diet.

5   Don't .... the animals as they may bite you !

Speaking

13 **Imagine you and your partner share a flat. Look at the television programmes for Sunday evening.**

Student A You have planned to watch *Roxanne* as your English language teacher is going to use the film for discussion in tomorrow's lesson.

Student B You have a friend who is very keen on snooker and whom you have invited round to watch this evening's sport programme. You have been looking forward to it all day.

SUNDAY TV

1

7.15 Roxanne
Romantic comedy, starring **Steve Martin, Daryl Hannah**
Nelson is a small town of attractive wooden houses, tree-lined streets and lush mountain views. The most spectacular view, however, is of the astonishingly large nose of Nelson's beloved fire chief C D Bales. His remarkable proboscis catches the whiff of love in the air when he encounters Roxanne Kowalski, but her affections lie with shy new fireman Chris in the mistaken belief that he has brains as well as brawn. So C D finds himself the unwilling go-between in this affair of the heart. Steve Martin also wrote the script, which is based on Edmond Rostand's classic play *Cyrano de Bergerac*.

Roxanne Steve Martin and Daryl Hannah in the fun update of romantic drama *Cyrano de Bergerac*

C D Bales...................... STEVE MARTIN
Roxanne .... DARYL HANNAH
Chris .... RICK ROSSOVICH
Dixie .... SHELLEY DUVALL
Chuck .... JOHN KAPELOS
Mayor Deebs .... FRED WILLARD
Dean .... MAX ALEXANDER
Andy .... MICHAEL J POLLARD
Ralston .... STEVE MITTLEMAN
Director Fred Schepisi (1987)
Stereo Subtitled 42604513

2

7.0-8.30 Snooker
UK Championship from the Guild Hall, Preston. Last year's finalists Stephen Hendry and Ronnie Sullivan should both be in action in tonight's third round. Commentary by Ted Lowe, Ray Edmonds, Clive Everton, John Virgo, John Spencer and Dennis Taylor.
Stereo 6756204

Stephen Hendry

EUROSPORT
8.30 Rallying Coverage of the Network Q RAC Rally. *9878*
9.00 Boxing Paul Weir takes on Narciso Rodriguez for the vacant WBO light flyweight world championship. *95192*
11.00 Equestrianism *94168*
12.00-12.30am Eurosport News Results roundup. *68347*

Try to persuade your partner to let you have your own way. Be ready to act out your dialogue for the class.
Use the following prompts to help you.

I'd like to watch … if you don't mind …	Would/Do you mind if … ?
I'm sorry, but …	I'd rather you didn't because …
Please let me …	Why don't you/we …
I'm afraid it's out of the question because …	Perhaps you/we could …

Speaking and Writing

14 **Imagine that you can choose five records, tapes or CDs and one book to take with you to a desert island. Write down your own choices, and then write down the questions you would ask to find out what at least four other people would choose and why.**

15 **Using the information you have collected, is there clearly a favourite piece of music or book which your friends have chosen ?**
Be ready to tell your teacher your results.

For Further Practice in writing turn to page 131.

Reading

16   Each month a well-known photographer chooses a photograph which she/he especially likes for a magazine called 'Photographer's News'. This month the photographer Ludmila Gregg writes about 'Street Scene'.

Photographer's Choice

Street Scene Spain, 1989 Filmer

I first saw 'Street Scene' hanging in a small gallery in the south west of England. The photograph was taken by Hardy Filmer whilst he was touring Spain in 1989 and one immediately recognises Filmer's eye for detail.

The picture is full of life and colour and I would guess had been taken fairly early in the day before the street became busy. Look carefully and you will see colourful clothes, skirts and dresses hanging up, people chatting, an elderly woman carrying a full shopping bag.

There is even a workman on a ladder; we have to decide for ourselves what he is doing: cleaning windows, watering plants or fixing something which we can't see!

What, one wonders, is the mood of the woman who is caught staring at the camera from behind the piles of melons, oranges, tomatoes and more. Or the thoughts of the woman who is sitting with her back to the wall and eating apricots?

I like the scene just as much for what it does tell us as for what it leaves to our imaginations.

Ludmila Gregg

Work in small groups of three or four. Look at the photograph and then read the text. Use a dictionary to help with any vocabulary you don't know. Then write down five questions which will check whether the text has been understood.

   Pass your questions to another group to answer. Make sure you know the answers to your own questions !

Reading

17 Work with a partner. Read these headlines.

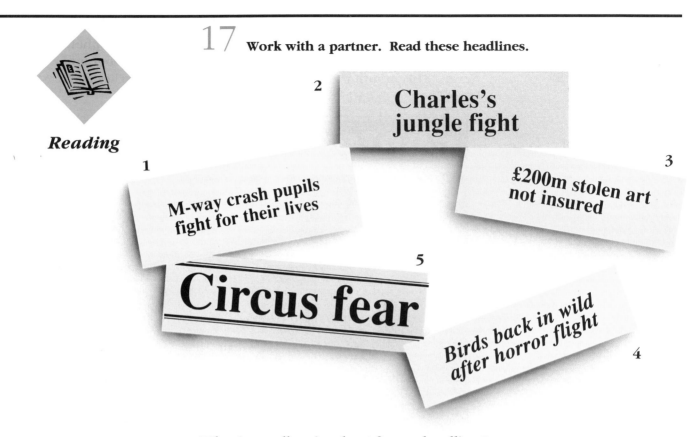

2 **Charles's jungle fight**

1 M-way crash pupils fight for their lives

3 £200m stolen art not insured

5 **Circus fear**

4 Birds back in wild after horror flight

What is usually missed out from a headline ?
Discuss with your partner what you think each headline might be about.
Rewrite each headline in sentence form.

18 Now look at the texts below. These are the opening paragraphs of each article.

A

WOULD-BE circus artists could be in trouble unless £40,000 can be found by early September.

B

THE DOZEN masterpieces stolen in the biggest art raid in American history were not insured.

C

THREE pupils are fighting for their lives after a motorway crash between a school minibus and a lorry in which a teenager died.

D

About 1,500 birds returned to freedom in their native country, equatorial Mali, after being saved by animal welfare officers when they arrived in a terrible state at a Belgian airport. They were among 5,500 sent there to be sold in pet shops.

E

PRINCE Charles is planning to make a private visit to one of Africa's last great rain forests in a personal bid to help halt its destruction.

Can you match each headline with its text ? Be ready to explain to your teacher how you matched them.

19 Work with your partner. Look at the advertisement for the opera 'Tornrak'.

☐ What language is the opera sung in ?
☐ When is it being performed ?
☐ Who wrote the opera ?

Listening

WEDNESDAY 4 JULY 7.15pm
WORLD PREMIERE

Tornrak

JOHN METCALF
Libretto by Michael Wilcox
Sung in English

Co-production with the Banff Centre, Canada

Conductor   Richard Armstrong
Producer   Mike Ashman
Set Designer   Bernard Culshaw
Costume Designer   John Pennoyer

Tornrak – the magical animal spirit which lives in all of us.

Welsh National
OPERA

SPECIAL OFFERS FOR

TORNRAK

A NEW OPERA BY JOHN METCALF

LIBRETTO BY MICHAEL WILCOX

BRISTOL HIPPODROME
(0272) 299444

WEDNESDAY
4 JULY 7.15PM

SPECIAL FAMILY OFFER
Two adults with
two children
£40.00
for best available seats

HALF PRICE
for
Under Eighteens
Students
Youth & Music Members

Opera	Date	Alt. Date	No of Tickets	First Choice Seat Location	Alternative Seat Location	Ticket Price	TOTAL	Box Office Use
Rosenkavalier								
Freischütz								
Cosi fan tutte								
Barber								
Otello								
Tornrak								
						TOTAL		

20 Now listen to two people who are discussing whether to book seats for 'Tornrak'. As you listen, fill in the booking form.

Speaking

21 **Work with your partner. Look at the advertisements for the musical 'Evita' and the ballet 'The Nutcracker'.**

You would like to see one of these but you can't afford more than £12 each for a ticket. Decide which one you would like to see together; work out the cost and then fill in the appropriate booking form.

KNOW YOUR VOCABULARY

22 **Know your way round a theatre.**

☐ What sign do you look for when you want to go in ?

☐ What sign do you look for when you want to leave ?

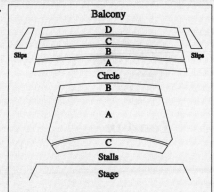

23 **Find out everything you can about this theatre ticket; get ready to tell your teacher.**

24 **Learn these words. Listen to your teacher and mark the main word stress(es).**

For example: picture

1 classical	5 audience	9 sculpture	13 screen
2 comedian	6 popular	10 antique	14 musical
3 musician	7 performance	11 opera	
4 interval	8 cloakroom	12 ballet	

25 **Write down your answers.**

1 What is your favourite form of entertainment ?

2 How much does a cinema ticket cost in your country ?

3 Which theatre would you recommend a foreigner to visit ?

4 Is your country famous for any particular form of entertainment ? If so, what is it called ?

9 Work, Sports, Hobbies

Lead-in

1 Work with a partner. Do you remember these faces from Unit 1 ?
Can you remember which countries they came from ?

Each person has a hobby. Can you guess who has which hobby ?

Listening

2 **Now listen to a teacher talking to some students about their hobbies. The students are called Jack, Sophie, Leo and Daniella.**

Look at the rows of pictures. Put a tick in the box under the correct picture for each student's hobby.

Jack's hobby ?

Sophie's hobby ?

Leo's hobby ?

Daniella's hobby ?

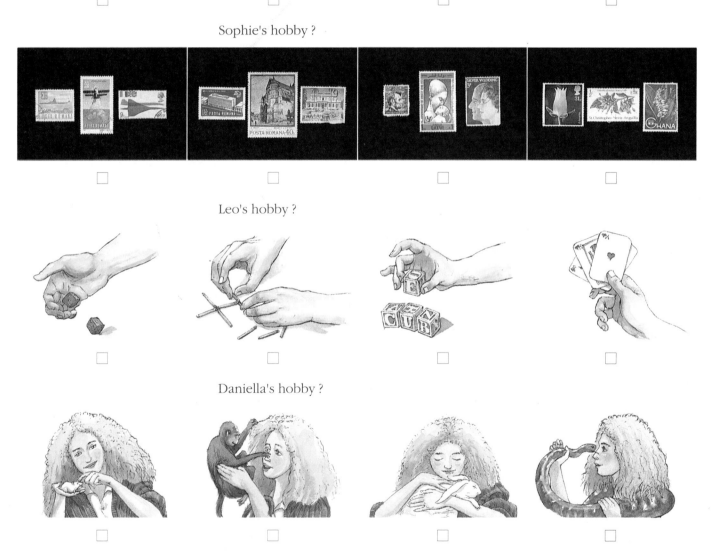

3 **Do you have a hobby ? Do you know anyone with an unusual hobby ? Find three people in your class with different hobbies. Be ready to tell your teacher about your friends' hobbies.**

Reading

4 **Robin Knox-Johnson is a famous yachtsman.**
Before you read the interview look at questions 1-6.

1   How old was Robin when he first became interested in boats ?
2   Why is it important to listen to weather forecasts ?
3   Does he ever feel afraid ?
4   Does he dislike being away from land ?
5   What is his favourite kind of music ?
6   What makes him feel young again ?

Now work with a partner. Read the text and see how quickly you can find the answers to the questions.

Seafaring tales

Nicki Silverman, 9, from London interviews round-the-world yachtsman and writer Robin Knox-Johnson.

INTERVIEWER: When did you first become interested in sailing?
Robin Knox-Johnson: When I was about eight years old. I bought my first boat when I was 14 and it sank!

I: What did you think about when you were on a long voyage?
RKJ: All sorts of things, but you know you're really quite busy because there's a lot of work to do, not just navigating - which means finding out where you are and working out the course of where you want to go to.

You have got to listen to the weather forecast and see what sort of weather is coming. You try to avoid the bad weather, you can't always do that, you've got to keep the boat going. There is always repairs and maintenance to do on the boat and I do quite a lot of writing when I am at sea. So you are really very busy.

I: Are you ever afraid when you go sailing a long way from land?
RKJ: It's not being a long way from land that makes you afraid. It's sometimes when you get a very, very rough sea and the boat is being thrown around like a cork on top of a big pond. Then you wonder if the boat is going to be alright, that's when you get a little bit afraid.

But I don't mind being away from land, that doesn't worry me. In fact it's nicer to be away from land, it's easier to sail - you've nothing to run into you see.

I: Have you ever got lost?
RKJ: Well it's rather hard to get lost when you're navigating. Providing you can see the sun, you can navigate.

I: When you go on a long voyage do you like listening to music and if so, what kind?
RKJ: Yes, I do like listening to music, I like it a lot and I play all sorts of music. Mainly classical music, but sometimes I like a little bit of rock and roll, it reminds me of when I was young, and I like musicals. So I play all sorts of music, but on balance, I suppose I favour classical music.

I: What is the most frightening thing that has happened to you while you have been on a long voyage?
RKJ: I think the most striking thing that has occurred was when I was going around the world on my own and I ran into very bad weather. I thought the boat was going to break up.

That was frightening.

5 Dame Judi Dench earns her living as an actress. Read what she says about herself and her life.

An acting life

by Emma Owczarski, from London

I MET Dame Judi Dench backstage at the Aldwych theatre where she is presently performing in *The Cherry Orchard*, by the Russian playwright Anton Chekov. I asked her some questions, and this is what she told me.

Judi Dench's family were not very rich, and because Judi's parents wanted her and her brother to have a good education, their father, who was a GP, worked extra hard and they gave up a lot of things.

Dame Judi went to a boarding school, and then to the Central School of Speech and Drama to train as a set designer. When she left Dame Judi went into acting because she thought she would not be a good set designer; she was also influenced by her brother who liked acting.

Dame Judi Dench started in show business at the age of 22, and this is her 33rd year in the theatre. Dame Judi told me she enjoyed working with her husband Michael, in *A Fine Romance* on television but she found it very strange being recorded with a live audience.

She is more used to doing things like Shakespeare. In her spare time Dame Judi likes sewing, tapestry, art, reading books and the *Early Times*, and also playing with her dolls' house, and just having a good time.

Now work with a partner. The interviewer had prepared a lot of questions but only had time to ask some of them. Put a tick in the box beside the questions which the interviewer asked.

1 ☐ Did you come from a family who had a lot of money ?
2 ☐ Is it true that you lived in India when you were a child ?
3 ☐ What was your father's job ?
4 ☐ What sort of school did you go to ?
5 ☐ What was the best family holiday you remember ?
6 ☐ Did you go into acting straight after leaving school ?
7 ☐ How old were you when you got married ?
8 ☐ How many children have you got ?
9 ☐ How many years have you worked in the theatre ?
10 ☐ What are your hobbies ?

Speaking

6 **Work with a partner. Are you still studying or have you already got a job? Would you be interested in any of these jobs? Why/ why not?**

SECRETARY

TRAINEE MANAGER

FULL-TIME PORTER

ENGINEER

NURSERY TEACHER

HAIRDRESSER

PART-TIME COOK

COMPUTER ASSISTANT

Reading

7 **Read the text below.**

SEVENTEEN-year-old business hotshot James Warren has gone for a more upmarket office.

He has moved his £1 million computer business from his bedroom into office space near his home in Sutton, Surrey.

Schoolboy James has built up a successful computer consultancy from his home. He has now be granted a year off from school to work on his business, and decided to move offices to give his company a more professional look.

What is special about James Warren ? Do you know anyone who has done something similar ?

Speaking

8   Work with a partner. Here is a list of jobs. Put them in order of best-paid and worst-paid depending on what you know about the job market in your own country. For example if you think a school teacher is the most highly paid put 1, and so on. In the second column put a letter A - E in order to show job satisfaction, using A to show the highest level of satisfaction.

	Pay	Job Satisfaction
Nurse		
Businessman/woman		
Policeman		
Office Worker		
Farmer		
Professional footballer		
Tourist guide		
House painter		
Factory worker		
School teacher		

9   Now compare your list with other students' lists.
   Do you think the pay which people receive for the jobs they do is always fair ? Are there many jobs which pay well and have a high level of satisfaction ?

Writing

10   If you apply for a job you may be asked for a CV or 'curriculum vitae'. This is a brief written account of your personal details, your education, and the jobs you have had.
   Write your own CV. Use the following headings to help you.

Name
Age
Date of birth
Address and telephone number
Married / single
Occupation
School / college / university attended (with dates)
Qualifications (with dates)
Work / job experience
Interests

Listening

11 **Look at these various sports. How many of them do you enjoy doing ? Or perhaps you're an 'armchair sports person' ?!**

Squash

Tennis

Swimming

Hockey

Hockey

Athletics

Cycling

Skiing

Basketball

Mountain biking

Gymnastics

Riding

Climbing

Soccer

Rugby

Cricket

Table Tennis

You are going to hear a radio sports report. As you listen, write down the name of each sport you hear mentioned.

At the end of the report you will hear some football results; try to write down the result of each match.

Sports mentioned:

....

....

Football results:

Belgium	____	Italy	____
Holland	____	Greece	____
Egypt	____	Scotland	____
France	____	Wales	____
Brazil	____	Argentina	____

For Further Practice in listening turn to page 132.

Speaking

12 Your teacher is going to organise a Balloon Debate.

Four people are flying high above the earth in a balloon. Unfortunately the balloon develops a tiny hole. In order to bring the balloon down safely three people have to be thrown overboard !

All the people in the balloon represent *either* a sport or a hobby *or* a famous sportswoman/man.

Choose *one* of these and write a short speech - about 50 words - saying why you think your choice of sport/hobby/sportswoman/man should stay in the balloon. The class will vote on what/who should be thrown overboard.

Begin your speech like this: 'I think you should vote for me because I represent ...'

Use the following structure to help you:

Without … people would/wouldn't …
If you throw me out …
If people can't play … they will/won't …
This sport/hobby is good for you because …

Try to think of some good reasons to persuade the class why you should stay in the balloon!

Grammar

▶   **PRESENT PERFECT TENSE**

13 The present perfect tense (simple) is formed like this: **has/have + past participle**. For example:

1   I have played football for 10 years.
2   Estella has not played hockey since 1988.

And the present perfect progressive form: has/have + been + verb base + -ing.

3   I've been learning English for many years.
4   What has he been doing all this time ?

This tense connects a point in the past with the present. For example, if you moved to your present house/apartment five years ago and you are still living there now, you would say:

5   'I've lived at this address for five years.'

There are a few adverbs which are commonly used with this tense (although they can be used with other tenses too, of course):

just / never / ever / already / yet

14 Work with a partner. In the dialogues below fill in the missing adverbs and then practise reading the sentences aloud to each other.

1 A: Have you .... been skiing ?
   B: Yes - I went to Austria a few years ago.
2 A: Have you phoned your parents .... ?
   B: No - every time I try somebody else is using the phone.
3 A: I haven't done my homework .... - it's too difficult !
   B: I know - I haven't done mine either !
4 A: I've .... ridden a horse, have you ?
   B: Only once and then I fell off !
5 A: Would you like a cup of coffee ?
   B: No thanks - I've .... finished one.
6 A: Would you like to come with me to see 'Driving Miss Daisy' - it's on at the cinema this week.
   B: I've .... seen it I'm afraid.
7 A: Did you enjoy the play ?
   B: Very much, I've .... laughed so much in all my life !
8 A: I've .... read a brilliant book about racing drivers - would you like to borrow it ?
   B: Oh yes please.

▶ **PRESENT PERFECT AND FOR, SINCE**

15 Look back at examples 1, 2, 3 and 5 in exercise 13. They all use the preposition for or since. For and since are very commonly used with the present perfect simple/progressive tense.

The present perfect + for **refers to a period of time, for example five years, ten minutes, a long time. It does not refer to a particular point in the past. For example:**

She's lived in Manchester for twenty years

The present perfect + since **refers to a particular point in the past, for example a date, a time or even something which happened in the past. For example:**

They've been good friends since the war

16 Fill in the gaps in the following sentences with either for or since

1 I've been waiting for a letter from my father .... weeks.
2 Jaime has lived in England .... 1974.
3 I've known Dr Ariel .... a very long time.
4 I haven't seen Emi .... her wedding.
5 She hasn't spoken to anyone .... the accident last month.

For Further Practice in grammar turn to page 132.

Reading

17   **Work with a partner. Look at texts A, B, C and D.**

WHEREVER YOU GO, FOLLOW THE COUNTRY CODE

Enjoy the countryside and respect its life and work
Guard against all risk of fire
Fasten all gates
Keep your dogs under close control
Keep to public paths across farmland
Use gates and stiles to cross fences, hedges and walls
Leave livestock, crops and machinery alone
Take your litter home
Help to keep all water clean
Protect wildlife, plants and trees
Take special care on country roads
Make no unnecessary noise

A

SWIMMING POOL USERS SAFETY CODE

1. SPOT THE DANGERS
Take care, swimming pools can be hazardous. Water presents a risk of drowning, and injuries can occur from hitting the hard surrounds, or from misuse of the equipment.

2 ALWAYS SWIM WITHIN YOUR ABILITY
Never swim after a heavy meal or after alcohol. Avoid holding your breath and swimming long distances under water. Be especially careful if you have a medical condition such as epilepsy, asthma, diabetes or a heart condition.

3 CHECK NEW PLACES
Every pool is different, so always make sure you know how deep the water is, and check for other hazards such as diving boards, water slides and steep slopes into deeper water etc.

4 TAKE SAFETY ADVICE
Follow advice provided for your and others' safety. Avoid unruly behaviour which can be dangerous: for instance, running on the side of the pool; ducking; acrobatics in the water; or shouting or screaming (which could distract attention from an emergency). Always do as the lifeguards say, and remember that a moment of foolish behaviour can cost a life.

5 LOOK OUT FOR YOURSELF AND OTHER SWIMMERS
If is safer to swim with a companion. Keep an eye open for others, particularly young children and non-swimmers.

6 LEARN HOW TO HELP
If you see somebody in difficulty, get help immediately. In an emergency, keep calm and do exactly as you are told.

B

LAKE USERS

Beware of the cold. Lake water does not rise in temperature like the sea.

Watch out for sudden changes in the weather.

Watch out for broken glass on the lake shore.

If you see anyone in difficulties notify the Police immediately. Go to the nearest telephone and dial 999.

C

WINTER WALKING

Some extra precautions are needed if you are to enjoy winter walking. Remember that daylight hours are shorter and walking conditions can be difficult. Your plan should not be too ambitious. Carry some extra clothing. In conditions of snow and ice each member of the party should carry an ice axe and know how to use it. Boots are essential for winter conditions, with soles and uppers which are rigid enough to prevent distorting on hard snow slopes.

D

1   What is the purpose of these texts ?
   ☐ to make the reader laugh
   ☐ to complain about people's behaviour
   ☐ to give people advice
   ☐ to give the writers' opinions
2   What is the subject of each text ?
3   Which text is for serious walkers ?
4   Is text B for swimmers or about water sports in general ?
5   Which texts tell you what to do in an emergency ?
6   Which text mentions animals ?
7   What is the difference between lake and sea water ?
8   What is the main reason for checking a new swimming pool ?

Speaking

18 Your teacher has been offered a picture for the classroom.

Bravo!

Shot!

Student A: You are very keen on tennis and want to persuade your teacher to buy 'Bravo!'.

Student B: You are crazy about golf and play in your spare time whenever you can. You want 'Shot!'.

Be ready with one sentence to persuade your teacher. Use the following prompts to help you:

'I think you should buy … - it's …'
'Why don't you buy … - it's …'
'You ought to buy … because …'
'Please will you buy … as …'

Writing

19 Work with a partner. Look at the pictures on the opposite page of the activities you can do at an Adventure Centre.

You are spending a week at this Adventure Centre and you have chosen to learn/practise three of these sports.

Now write a letter to your English language teacher telling her/him about what you are doing and whether you are enjoying yourself. Remember to say something about the food and accommodation as well as the sports activities. Write about 100 words.

Begin like this:

Dear ....
I am spending a week at an Adventure Centre in ....
....

KNOW YOUR VOCABULARY

20 What are these people doing ?

jog
kick
relax
do exercises
throw

21 Do you know what these symbols mean ?

$$+ \quad - \quad \times \quad \div \quad = \quad \%$$

22 Do you know the English words for these punctuation marks ?

" " . ; ( ) ! 's , : ? -

23 Do you know what these abbreviations are short for ?

AD	BC	cont'd	km.	min.	PTO	St.
am	c/o	dep.	Ltd.	NB	Rd.	Xmas
arr.	cm.	gm.	max.	pp	Sq.	yr.

24 Learn these words. Listen to your teacher and mark the main word stress(es).

For example: burglar

1 guard	3 stadium	5 hydrofoil	7 army	9 duvet
2 detective	4 electronic	6 hovercraft	8 receptionist	10 hijack

10 Practice Test

Reading

PART 1

Questions 1–5
- Look at the sign in each question.
- Someone asks you what it means.
- Mark the letter next to the correct explanation – **A, B, C** or **D** – **on your answer sheet.**

Example:

A The next phone is four miles away.
B There are four phones on this motorway.
C There is a phone every four miles.
D This motorway phone is number four.

Example answer:

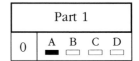

Part 1				
0	A	B	C	D

1

CHILDREN
are not allowed
into the exhibition
without an adult

A Children pay half price to see this exhibition.
B Children must wait outside for their parents.
C Children can go into the exhibition in groups.
D Children cannot go alone to this exhibition.

2

When you have
finished,
please leave
the table
for other passengers.

Thank you.

A You can stay here as long as you wish.
B This table is reserved for special passengers.
C You are asked to go when your meal is over.
D This table is for people who do not smoke.

3

To reserve a room,
please contact the hotel directly
during reception opening hours.

A Reservations can be made through a travel agency.
B The reservation desk is open 24 hours a day.
C Reservations must be booked through the hotel.
D The hotel reception does not handle group reservations.

4

> WARNING
> Cross only when
> lights show

A You can cross when the lights are on.
B It is unsafe to cross by these lights.
C You cannot cross here without a ticket.
D It is safe to cross when the lights are off.

5

> When you are shopping
> take one to the store
> if you wish

A You must use a trolley in the store.
B You may help yourself to a trolley.
C Please take your trolley with you.
D Please leave your trolley at the store.

PART 2

Questions 6–10

- The people below are looking for somewhere to stay on holiday.
- On the opposite page there are advertisements for holiday accommodation in South West Cornwall.
- Decide which accommodation **(letters A-H)** would be the most suitable for each group of people **(numbers 6-10).**
- For each of those numbers **mark the correct letter on your answer sheet.**

Example answer:

	Part 2							
0	A	B	C	D	E	F	G	H
	■	☐	☐	☐	☐	☐	☐	☐

6

The Jameson family want somewhere for up to five people close to the sea where they can look after themselves and their cat!

7

Mr and Mrs Eliot and their three children enjoy shopping, and being near a town centre is more important than being near the coast. They would prefer private accommodation to a hotel.

8

The Austen family have a friend from Germany with them and they want to stay somewhere peaceful (not a hotel), where they can be sure that their two dogs will be all right as well.

9

The Brooks want somewhere their young children can play safely (not near water!), and away from animals. They don't want to travel at a weekend.

10

Keith and Erika are planning to go away in December for a short break. They want to find a hotel which is not too big and which offers good food.

A

MRS. T. ADDISON

2 Brook Close, Helston, Cornwall
TR13 8NY Tel: (01326) 562846
Bed & Breakfast in private house. Two
bedrooms, one double, one single, both with
H&C, shaver sockets & central heating. Guests
own shower & toilet. Animals welcome. Parking.

B

The **Penmenner House Hotel** invites you to enjoy a
carefree, relaxing holiday set amidst the magnificent
coastal scenery of Britain's most southerly point.

We offer comfortable, en-suite, sea view bedrooms;
good food on the table; fine wine in the cellar; logs on
the fire; peace, quiet and a special welcome – it all
adds up to friendly hospitality. Spanish and German
spoken.

Open Apr. – Oct.   Tel: (01524) 629718

C

GLENBRACKEN HOUSE
PORTREATH

3 bedroom detached holiday home. Sleeps 6, just a
few minutes walk to the beach, shops and harbour.
For further details please send SAE to: Mrs A.D.
Tregloan, Bodilly Farm, Trenear, Helston
TR13 0HA Tel: (01326) 572112

D

BOAK HOUSE COVERACK

Overlooks cove. Sea views from all four bedrooms.
TV lounge, home cooking. Children welcome.
Fresh farm produce. Safe bathing, windsurfing,
fishing trips. Personal supervision.
Terms: from £70.00 per week.
Details: Mrs Wendy Watters, Boak House, Coverack,
Helston, Cornwall. Tel: St. Keverne (01326) 280608

E

Unwind in the peace of
POLCOVERACK!

Seven comfortable stone-built cottages,
immaculately maintained on attractive coastal farm,
1/2 mile beach and unspoilt fishing village.
Friendly atmosphere: real relaxation for grown-ups,
as children can enjoy many countryside activities
in traffic-free safety. Weekday changeovers.
Sorry no pets!
Telephone: (01326) 280497

F

SECLUDED DETACHED SELF-CATERING
BUNGALOW

Garage & Parking. Walled gardens to front and rear.
Pleasant & quiet. Three miles to coast and beaches.
Walking distance to Redruth town centre. Touring
centre for Cornwall. Sleeps 4/6. Brochure with
pleasure: Mrs. S. Rilstone, (The Retreat), Pentreve,
Wheal Leisure, Perranporth, Cornwall TR6 0EY
Telephone: (01872) 572157

G

Mounts Bay House Hotel
The Lizard
Cornwall TR12 7NP

Small hotel in own grounds with superb view
of Kynance Cove. Friendly relaxed atmosphere.
Cosy bar. Tempting choice of menu.
Open all year. Pets welcome.
Grace & Sam Crossley Tel: (01326) 290305

AA Listed   English Tourist Board   RAC Listed

Access/Visa accepted.

H

Crossroads Motel
BEDROOMS
*Our forty, mainly double and twin-bedded
rooms are all furnished with TVs, private
bathrooms, direct self-dial telephone, tea-
making facilities and enjoy full central
heating.*
Scorrier, Redruth, Cornwall TR15 5BP
Telephone: (01209) 820551
*Situated at Scorrier exit off A30 2 miles east
of Redruth, 6 miles from Truro.*

PART 3

Questions 11–20

- Look at the statements below about post services.
- Read the text on the opposite page to decide if each statement is correct or incorrect.
- If it is correct, **mark A on your answer sheet.**
- If it is not correct, **mark B on your answer sheet.**

Example answer:

Part 3		
0	A ▬	B ▭

11 For more information you can write to RMP.

12 RMP will only deliver in certain special areas.

13 The RMP delivery service usually takes four days in the UK.

14 Standard Service offers the fastest delivery time.

15 Weekend delivery costs are the same as weekday.

16 Datapost promise that mail posted one day will arrive the next.

17 International Parcelforce offers three different services.

18 International Standard Service is faster than the Economy Service.

19 Completing customs forms applies to all countries.

20 There are two phone numbers to ring for more information on when parcels are delivered.

A FAMILIAR SERVICE GETS A NEW NAME

Royal Mail Parcels has got a bright new name.

Royal Mail Parcelforce.

But we have much more than a new name to offer you. We're now a separate organisation, with our own way of doing things.

And we give *you* the choice about how fast you want your parcel delivered and how much you want to pay. Our services are listed opposite – choose the one that's right for you.

To find out more about how we can help you, just ask at a post office counter.

It's your choice.

Trust Royal Mail Parcelforce to deliver your parcels. We call at every single UK address, and you know you're in safe and friendly hands.

Nationwide delivery normally takes up to 3 days. And when you're sending parcels abroad, you can choose the service that suits your budget best.

But if it can't wait ... choose Datapost. We'll rush your parcel across the country by the very next day – and to the other side of the world faster than you'd ever think possible.

Details of our services are listed below. And remember, only Royal Mail Parcelforce can offer you all this choice.

Royal Mail Parcelforce

Standard Service
Delivery normally within 3 days to every address in the UK. Saturday delivery at no extra charge.

Datapost
Guaranteed 10am next-day delivery to all major UK towns, and by noon to almost everywhere else.

Royal Mail Parcelforce International

Parcelforce has access to the world's largest delivery network – reaching over 214 different countries and territories. Parcelforce gives you a choice of 3 international services:

For all urgent parcels and documents ...

International Datapost
* Guaranteed express deliveries to over 170 countries and territories.

For less urgent deliveries ...

International Standard Service
* Europe from five working days, the rest of the world from seven working days;

International Economy Service
* Europe from 10 working days, the rest of the world from 20 working days.

At Parcelforce we always try to keep paperwork to a minimum.

You no longer have to fill in a customs form about the weight and value of a parcel's contents for any EC country.

For more information on delivery times you can call us free on 0800 246 246.

If you would like copies of Parcelforce guides to International services – or any other advice call us free on 0800 641 146.

PART 4

Questions 21–25

- Read the text and questions below.
- For each question, mark the letter next to the correct answer – **A, B, C** or **D** – **on your answer sheet.**

Example answer:

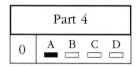

Part 4	
0	A ■ B ▭ C ▭ D ▭

Consulates exist to help citizens abroad to help themselves. Every year millions of people go abroad for pleasure or profit. There are consular officers ready to do what they can to help if people get into difficulties, but for all sorts of reasons there are limits to what they can do. Most times things go well for travellers abroad but occasionally things go wrong.

So, whether you are an experienced traveller or a first timer, going by yourself, with the family or a group there are things you should do before you go. Think about money and tickets well in advance. Take enough money including enough to pay your return fare, and hold on to it. Better still, buy return tickets in the first place. In an emergency a consul will contact relatives or friends and ask them to help you with money or tickets. But there's no law that says a consul has to lend you money and if he eventually does (and it will have to be repaid) he will want to be satisfied first that you really do have no money and there is no one else you know who can help.

It is also important to take out proper insurance for everything from car breakdowns to loss of life. A consul cannot pay your medical or any other bills, nor can he do the work of local travel representatives or motoring organisations.

21 What is the author trying to do in the text?

A inform people about laws abroad

B describe an international problem

C explain how to visit a consulate

D give advice about consulates

22 Why would somebody read the text?

A to know how to contact a consul

B to find out how to make a complaint

C to know when to contact a consul

D to find out where a consul lives

23 Travellers should try and buy a return ticket in case they

A become short of money.

B get into difficulties.

C lose their documents.

D become seriously ill.

24   You can borrow money from a consul if you

    A   need to stay abroad longer.

    B   have to help a relative.

    C   have no other financial means.

    D   need to have your car repaired.

25   Which of the following notices would you see in a Consular Office?

CONSULAR OFFICE

In an emergency you may contact your consul. He may give you advice but you should not rely on being given financial help.

A

CONSULAR OFFICE

In an emergency you may contact this office. Your consul can always help with hospital and dental costs.

B

CONSULAR OFFICE

You may contact your consul if you have run out of money. He will arrange for you to receive help if you cannot pay your bills.

C

CONSULAR OFFICE

Your consul is here to help you. If your car has broken down or you are experiencing travel difficulties of any kind, contact your consul.

D

PART 5

Questions 26–35

● Read the text below and choose the correct word for each space.
● For each question, mark the letter next to the correct word – **A, B, C** or **D** – on **your answer sheet.**

Example answer:

	Part 5
0	A ■ B ▭ C ▭ D ▭

It was in 1819, in Vevey, **(0)** .... Francois-Louis Cailler set up a small business making and selling cocoa and chocolate **(26)** .... eventually became the first Swiss chocolate factory. Handmade chocolate was **(27)** .... made in other countries **(28)** .... Cailler was the first to **(29)** .... the idea of making chocolate by machine. The business developed and in 1898, Alexander Cailler, **(30)** .... grandson, left Vevey and built a new factory at Broc in the heart **(31)** .... the Gruyère district, an area well-known **(32)** .... the richness of its milk. The following year **(33)** .... were 120 workers at the factory and by 1906 over a thousand people **(34)** .... employed there. By this time the chocolate industry had **(35)** .... an important part of the Swiss economy.

0	**A** that	**B** while	**C** as	**D** when
26	**A** who	**B** which	**C** it	**D** what
27	**A** yet	**B** now	**C** already	**D** even
28	**A** but	**B** because	**C** so	**D** for
29	**A** think	**B** have	**C** put	**D** show
30	**A** its	**B** their	**C** his	**D** whose
31	**A** at	**B** by	**C** up	**D** of
32	**A** for	**B** with	**C** in	**D** to
33	**A** it	**B** there	**C** they	**D** those
34	**A** had	**B** been	**C** were	**D** was
35	**A** turned	**B** grown	**C** found	**D** become

Writing

PART 1

Questions 1–5
- Here are some sentences about studying music.
- For each question, finish the second sentence so that it means the same as the first.
- The second sentence is started for you. **Write only the missing words on your answer sheet.**
- You may use this page for any rough work.

Example: Musical instruments are very expensive.

Musical instruments cost *a lot of money.* ....

1   There are many different kinds of colleges in Britain.

Britain ....

2   Music is taught in just a few colleges.

Just a few colleges ....

3   You must be able to play at least two instruments.

It is ....

4   Some students are frightened of playing in public.

Playing ....

5   Teaching music is preferable for these students.

These students ....

PART 2

Questions 6–15

● You are looking for a holiday job for next year.
● Camp Australia has sent you this application form.
● Fill in the form and answer each question.
● **Write your answers on your answer sheet.**
● You may use this page for any rough work.

Come and work for us and we'll pay your air fare to Australia! **Camp Australia** needs young people willing to work in its summer camps with Australian children aged 8-13 years. A marvellous opportunity for work and holiday!

Application Form
CAMP AUSTRALIA SUMMER CAMPS

SURNAME **(6)** ....

FIRST NAME(S) **(7)** ....

HOME ADDRESS **(8)** ....

NATIONALITY **(9)** ....

DATE OF BIRTH (day/month/year) **(10)** ....

SEX **(11)** ....

How many weeks can you work?

(12) ....

What sport(s) can you play?

(13) ....

Why do you want to work for Camp Australia?

(14) ....

SIGNATURE

(15) ....

PART 3

Question 16

- You are spending a week's holiday at an activity camp.
- Write a letter to an English-speaking friend.
- Describe what you are doing and explain that you are finding some parts of the week's programme rather boring.
- **Finish the letter on your answer sheet, using about 100 words.**
- You may use this page for any rough work.

Activity Camp

August 7th

Dear ....,

    I am spending a week at this activity camp. ....

....

....

....

....

....

....

....

....

....

....

Listening

PART 1

Questions 1–7

● There are seven questions in this part.
● For each question there are four pictures and a short recording.
● You will hear each recording twice.
● For each question, look at the pictures and listen to the recording.
● Choose the correct picture and put a tick (✔) in the box below.

Example: What time is the film?

  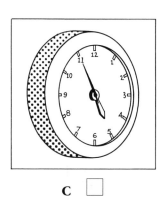 

A ✔   B ☐   C ☐   D ☐

1 What did the man buy?

A ☐   B ☐   C ☐   D ☐

2 Where will the man wait?

A ☐   B ☐   C ☐   D ☐

3   How did they spend their holiday?

A ☐   B ☐   C ☐   D ☐

4   Which is the woman's luggage?

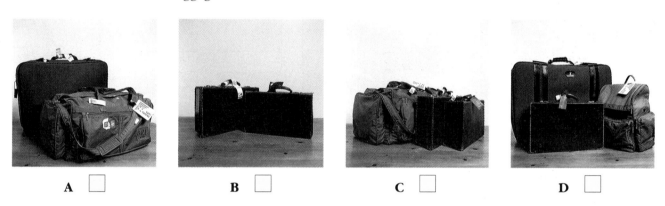

A ☐   B ☐   C ☐   D ☐

5   Which picture shows where the man was sitting?

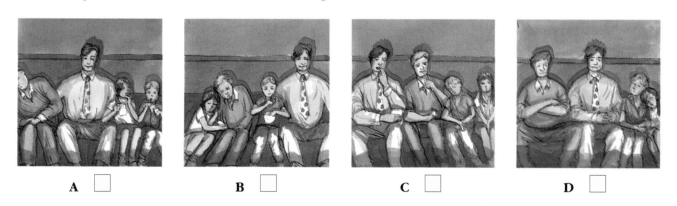

A ☐   B ☐   C ☐   D ☐

6   Which watch does the girl ask for?

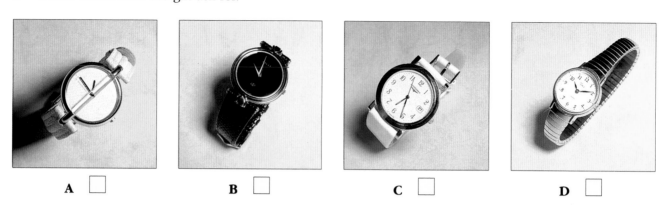

A   ☐   B   ☐   C   ☐   D   ☐

7   Where is the bank?

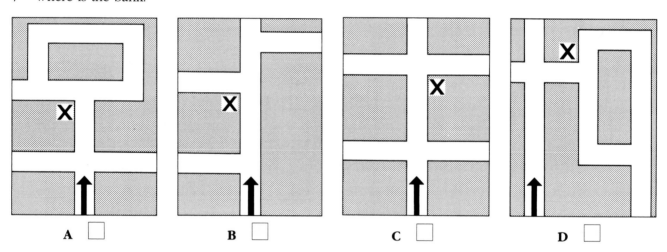

A   ☐   B   ☐   C   ☐   D   ☐

PART 2

Questions 8–13

- Look at the questions for this part.
- You will hear part of a radio programme about travel and weather.
- Put a tick (✔) in the correct box for each question.

8   Queues on the motorway are due to

- **A** ☐ a road crash.
- **B** ☐ bad weather.
- **C** ☐ a plane crash.
- **D** ☐ road works.

9   Some passengers flying from Heathrow have

- **A** ☐ spent the night at the airport.
- **B** ☐ decided to return home.
- **C** ☐ had to use another airport.
- **D** ☐ been sent to a nearby hotel.

10   Trains from London to Edinburgh are

- **A** ☐ delayed by fog.
- **B** ☐ extremely busy.
- **C** ☐ fully booked.
- **D** ☐ running late.

11   Passengers using the ferry can sail at

- **A** ☐ 11.00am.
- **B** ☐ 1.30pm.
- **C** ☐ 3.00pm.
- **D** ☐ 3.30pm.

12   For information on sailings ring

- **A** ☐ 057 4191.
- **B** ☐ 075 4914.
- **C** ☐ 057 4419.
- **D** ☐ 075 4491.

13   There are fewer coaches because of

- **A** ☐ poor weather.
- **B** ☐ drivers being ill.
- **C** ☐ engine breakdowns.
- **D** ☐ crowded motorways.

PART 3

Questions 14–19
- Look at the notes about a public meeting.
- Some information is missing.
- You will hear a person talking about saving a local hospital.
- For each question, fill in the missing information in the numbered space.

Public Meeting : SAVE OUR HOSPITAL

* (14).................... is what we need most!

for : advertising

   printing posters

   (15).................... and badges

* suggestions : organise a (16)....................

                        or a (17)....................

* can have the school hall without paying!

* 3 months from now : (18)....................

   necessary to contact papers, radio

   and TV

* Committee want suggestions over

   (19)....................

PART 4

Questions 20–25

- Look at the six statements for this part.
- You will hear a conversation between a man and a woman about moving house.
- Decide if you think each statement is correct or incorrect.
- If you think it is correct, put a tick (✔) in the box under **A** for **YES**. If you think it is not correct, put a tick (✔) in the box under **B** for **NO.**

		A YES	B NO
20	The woman is keen on moving.	☐	☐
21	The man has been reading while she's been talking.	☐	☐
22	The man agrees that their flat is small.	☐	☐
23	The man likes their flat because it's quiet.	☐	☐
24	The woman persuades the man to look at a house.	☐	☐
25	The man changes his mind about moving.	☐	☐

Further Practice

1 People and Places

Writing

You are hoping to study at a college in the UK for one year. Fill in the form below with your personal details.

Woodford College

Surname/Family name: ....

Other names: .... Sex: ....

Address: ....

....

Nationality: .... Date of Birth: ....

Occupation: ....

Have you any brothers or sisters? ....

How did you hear about the college? ....

....

....

Do you want us to arrange accommodation for you? (please tick)

       Yes ☐

       No ☐

Do you smoke?   Yes ☐

       No ☐

Have you any special requests? eg. food, religion ....

....

....

Signature .... Date ....

Grammar

Reported speech: **Finish the second sentence so that it has the same meaning as the first.**

1 'How old are you ?' Juan asked Maria.
Juan asked ....

2 'What do you do in your free time, Maria ?' asked Juan.
Juan asked ....

3 'When did you arrive in England ?' Maria asked Juan.
Maria asked ....

4 'I miss my family,' said Maria.
Maria said ....

5 'I want to be an interpreter when I grow up,' Maria said.
Maria said ....

6 'Do you want to be an interpreter too ?' Maria asked Juan.
Maria asked ....

Writing

Look at these leaflets.

You and a friend are spending a month in the UK on different language courses in different cities. Choose one of the leaflets and write a short letter (about 50 words) to your friend. Mention where you would like to go and some days and dates when you are free, and what time and where to meet.

2 Homes

Look at these notices and signs.

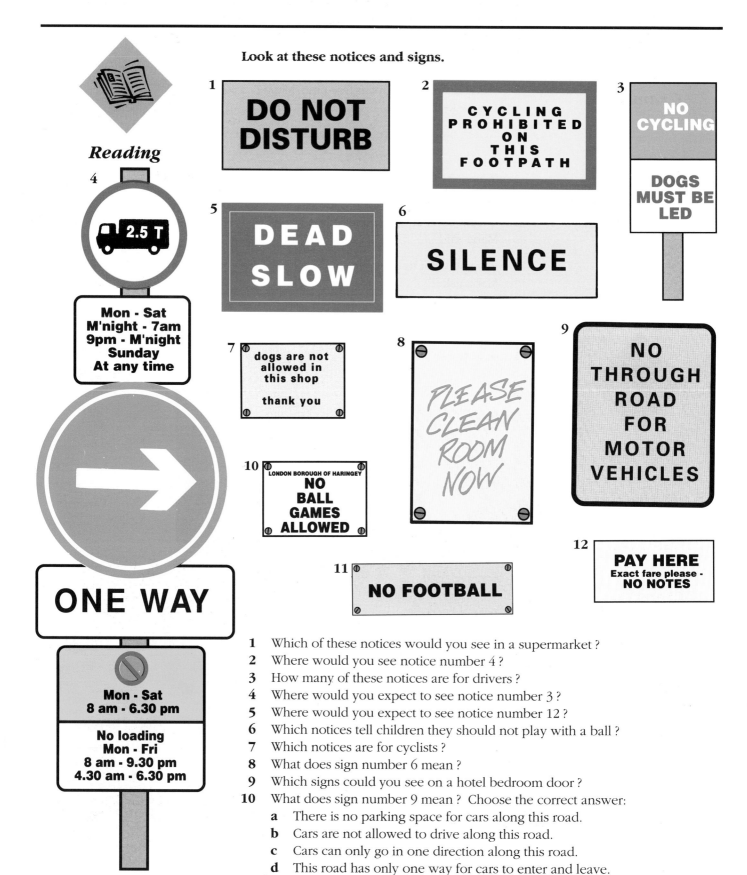

Reading

1 DO NOT DISTURB

2 CYCLING PROHIBITED ON THIS FOOTPATH

3 NO CYCLING / DOGS MUST BE LED

4 2.5 T / Mon - Sat M'night - 7am 9pm - M'night Sunday At any time

5 DEAD SLOW

6 SILENCE

7 dogs are not allowed in this shop / thank you

8 PLEASE CLEAN ROOM NOW

9 NO THROUGH ROAD FOR MOTOR VEHICLES

10 LONDON BOROUGH OF HARINGEY / NO BALL GAMES ALLOWED

11 NO FOOTBALL

12 PAY HERE / Exact fare please - NO NOTES

ONE WAY

Mon - Sat 8 am - 6.30 pm

No loading Mon - Fri 8 am - 9.30 pm 4.30 am - 6.30 pm

1 Which of these notices would you see in a supermarket ?
2 Where would you see notice number 4 ?
3 How many of these notices are for drivers ?
4 Where would you expect to see notice number 3 ?
5 Where would you expect to see notice number 12 ?
6 Which notices tell children they should not play with a ball ?
7 Which notices are for cyclists ?
8 What does sign number 6 mean ?
9 Which signs could you see on a hotel bedroom door ?
10 What does sign number 9 mean ? Choose the correct answer:
   a   There is no parking space for cars along this road.
   b   Cars are not allowed to drive along this road.
   c   Cars can only go in one direction along this road.
   d   This road has only one way for cars to enter and leave.

Writing

Look at these photographs. Your bedsit is in this house. Write another letter to your friend describing the kind of building you are living in and the surrounding area. The letter has been started for you. You should write about 100 words.

Dear ....
   I've been here a month now and I feel as if I've been here for years. Everyone is very friendly. I wish you could see the house where I live. It's on a very quiet road with lots of trees. ....
....

3 Shopping

Reading

Read the article below and circle the letter next to the word that best fits each space.

Example: Could you .... me some money please ?

A borrow   **B** help   **C** manage   **(D)** lend

Shopping in Mappstone is a must if you are visiting the area. There
(1) .... many shops and services all within walking distance
(2) .... the central square. The city is particularly busy during
(3) .... summer months of June, July and August when tourists visit
Mappstone from all over the (4) .... One of the main streets off the
central square - Cedar Avenue - is the most popular shopping area for not
(5) .... visitors but residents too. Stores line both sides of the avenue
and often (6) .... open late into the evening. Most of the shops in this
avenue are small and expensive (7) .... in nearby streets shoppers can
find almost anything at more reasonable (8) .... Tourists will find that
many of these shops offer an export service and goods (9) .... be
posted direct to the buyer's home country. Shops are usually closed on
Mondays but otherwise open from 9am in the morning (10) .... 8pm in
the evening.

1	**A** is	**B** are	**C** have	**D** be
2	**A** of	**B** in	**C** by	**D** to
3	**A** some	**B** a	**C** the	**D** one
4	**A** earth	**B** ground	**C** space	**D** world
5	**A** same	**B** just	**C** exactly	**D** very
6	**A** stay	**B** go	**C** make	**D** put
7	**A** since	**B** so	**C** but	**D** because
8	**A** costs	**B** numbers	**C** values	**D** prices
9	**A** can	**B** would	**C** might	**D** should
10	**A** with	**B** up	**C** until	**D** for

Speaking

Work with a partner using role cards A and B. You and a friend are spending six months studying in the UK. You have been given £20 to spend on buying some basic things for the kitchen in the flat which you are going to share. Look at the list of things and the prices and decide together how to spend the money. For example:

I think we need … because …
We must buy a/some … because …
I'd like to buy …

I don't agree, I think we should …
I prefer to spend the money on …
I don't want to buy …

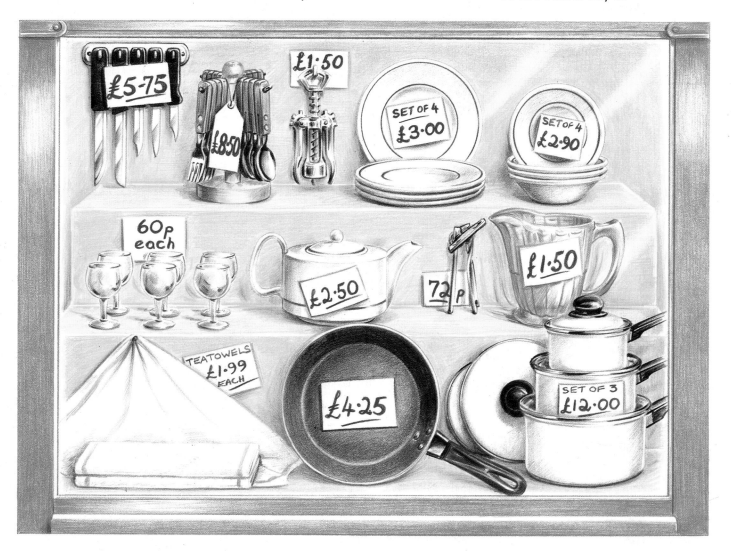

Role card A
You are not interested in cooking and would like to eat out in restaurants so you don't really want to spend any of this money on these things. You have other ideas !

Role card B
You like cooking and want to buy as many things as you possibly can for the £20 so you can prepare all the meals together.

4 Food and Drink

Listening

Put a tick in the box under the picture which you think is correct.

1   What will you find in the High Street?

 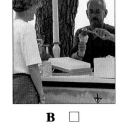  

A ☐   B ☐   C ☐   D ☐

2   What do they order?

A ☐   B ☐   C ☐   D ☐

3   What has the customer brought back?

 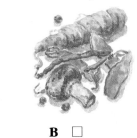  

A ☐   B ☐   C ☐   D ☐

4   What is the complaint about?

A ☐   B ☐   C ☐   D ☐

5   What does the man buy?

A ☐   B ☐   C ☐   D ☐

Writing

Read the instructions for the competition below.

COMPETITION

1. Choose a cook or chef for whom you would like to cook. This might be someone who owns or runs a restaurant; an hotel or restaurant chef; a television or theatre cook; a cookery author or journalist; or perhaps someone you know who is a very good cook.

and

2. Plan a two course menu around your chosen 'cookery guest'. Make your menu as imaginative as possible using a little original thought to make it special.

and

3. Tell us who your 'cookery guest' is and, in no more than 50 words, say why you would like this person as your guest.

and

4. Invent a new burger! Tell us what you would put inside a completely original burger bun. And give your invention a name. No more than 30 words but you can include a labelled drawing if you like.

Begin your competition entry like this:

I would like to cook a meal for … because …
I'd offer her/him a choice of …
…
My new burger is called ……………
It consists of …

UNIT 2   Exercise 23   *Student A*

5 *Health and Lifestyles*

Reading

Look at the five pictures. Someone asks you what each notice means. For each notice put a tick in one of the boxes to show the correct answer.

1

☐ You should get new glasses.
☐ Have your car brakes checked !
☐ Take care crossing roads.
☐ Have your eyes checked !

2

JUNIOR Kwells
WORK FAST ON TRAVEL SICKNESS
melt-in-the-mouth tablets

☐ Take these tablets if you have a headache.
☐ Take these tablets if you feel ill travelling.
☐ Take these tablets if you cannot sleep at night.
☐ Take these tablets if you are nervous of travelling.

3

TAKE CARE
Home accidents spell danger: they mean twice as much danger to elderly ladies as to elderly gentlemen – ladies look out!

☐ More road accidents happen to men than women.
☐ Women have more accidents at home than men.
☐ Men and women have more accidents at home than outside.
☐ More accidents happen to children at home than outside.

4

While you are abroad
Personal hygiene is vital

Always wash your hands before eating or handling food, particularly if you are camping or caravanning

☐ It is best to stay in a hotel when you are abroad.
☐ Cleanliness is very important when you are abroad.
☐ Avoid eating unwashed fruit when you are abroad.
☐ Make sure you buy bottled water when you are abroad.

5

APPOINTMENT CARD

If the doctor tells you to come again, you must see the clerk at the Reception Desk who will give you a time and date for your next attendance.

☐ Always make sure you see the clerk before you leave the hospital.
☐ The doctor will give you your next appointment.
☐ The clerk will send you the details of your next appointment.
☐ Only see the clerk if you are told to return by the doctor.

Look at the statements numbered 1 - 8 and then read the leaflet about the services for disabled passengers offered by British Airways. If you agree with a statement put a tick under True. If you disagree put a tick under False.

Reading

BRITISH AIRWAYS

TRAVEL WISE

INCAPACITATED PASSENGERS

PASSENGERS WITH MOBILITY DIFFICULTIES

● If you have mobility difficulties please ask about our wheelchair service and expert lifting facility. This is bookable in advance at no extra charge.

● Our Boeing 747 aircraft will carry a wheelchair on board for your use in the passenger cabin.

PASSENGERS WITH MEDICAL CONDITIONS BUT NOT DISABLED

● Passengers with medical conditions e.g. heart disease, breathing difficulties etc. but who are not disabled are recommended to ask for advice about travelling arrangements and to tell their Airline or Travel Agent of their medical condition.

● British Airways Medical Service offers a 24 hour advisory facility to all passengers, Doctors and other Health Care professionals on all aspects of air travel. The number is (081) 750 5616.

● If you need a special seat for medical reasons e.g. a seat near the toilet or in the no-smoking area, please ask when you make your booking.

● Oxygen sets can be provided at no extra charge if the use of oxygen is advised.

PASSENGERS WHO ARE ILL

● Passengers who are ill and are travelling for treatment, or are returning home for treatment will require medical clearance by British Airways. Free advice on the most suitable way to travel e.g. in a normal seat or on a stretcher, is available.

● Please tell us or your Travel Agent about your circumstances - so that everything can be done to help you.

PASSENGERS WHO ARE DISABLED

● Additionally we can simplify travel for disabled passengers by issuing free of charge a Frequent Travellers Card (FREMEC). The British Airways card is also accepted by most other major airlines.

● Disabled passengers can be escorted through departure and arrival controls.

OTHER FACILITIES

● Seeing-eye dogs for blind passengers travel free of charge in the United Kingdom and Ireland provide the animal is a trained Guide dog.

Travel wise with British Airways - Have a good journey.

Published by British Airways Customer Services Comet House (S25) London Heathrow Airport   M3511st

		True	*False*
1	You are not allowed to take your wheelchair on the plane.	____	____
2	You can reserve a particular seat if you need to.	____	____
3	You should tell your travel agent if you have a health problem.	____	____
4	Ordinary travellers can telephone BA for medical advice.	____	____
5	Oxygen sets are supplied free if required.	____	____
6	If you are ill you will not be allowed to fly without a doctor.	____	____
7	The British Airways FREMEC card cannot be used with other airlines.	____	____
8	Blind passengers' guide dogs are allowed to travel anywhere in the world.	____	____

6 Holidays and Travel

Reading and Writing

Look at the advertisement for The State House hotel at Land's End.

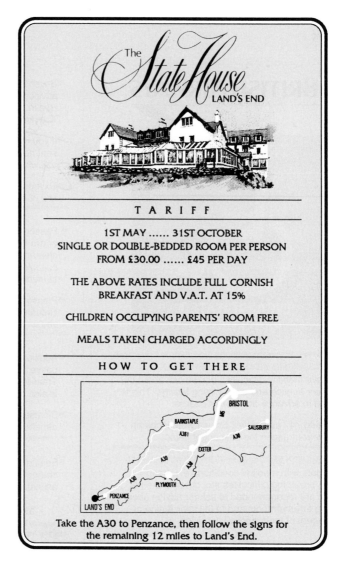

You and a friend want to book a few days' holiday at The State House hotel. Write a letter to the manager. (You do not need to include your address.)

Reading

Read the text below and circle the letter next to the word that best fits each space.

Example: At busy times it may be difficult to get a .... on some flights.

A place   **B** chair   Ⓒ seat   **D** room

BRITISH AIRWAYS

TRAVEL WISE

TRAVELLING AS AN ELDERLY PASSENGER

If you are not as young as you were and are travelling by air, we hope to make your journey more comfortable and trouble free (1) . . . . the following advice.

● If you (2) . . . . medicines or drugs make sure that you have enough with you for your time away.

● Please tell whoever makes your booking (3) . . . . you are on a special diet. We have a range of special meals available on most flights, just give us 24 hours to provide them.

● If you need (4) . . . . special seat, for example, in the smoking area or near the toilet, do (5) . . . . whoever makes your reservation or the person who checks you in for your flight at the airport.

● Airports often mean walking fairly (6) . . . . distances. If you find this difficult please let us know so that we (7) . . . . arrange to transport you to and from the aircraft (8) . . . . arrival and departure.

● If you need our help to reach your seat on the aircraft, please let us know (9) . . . . that we can take you on board before other passengers.

● We suggest you wear loose clothing especially if you are taking a long flight as (10) . . . . clothes become uncomfortable.

Do remember to tell us if you change your travel arrangements.

1	**A**	with	**B**	in	**C**	since	**D**	for
2	**A**	bring	**B**	take	**C**	hold	**D**	set
3	**A**	as	**B**	so	**C**	because	**D**	if
4	**A**	this	**B**	the	**C**	a	**D**	that
5	**A**	speak	**B**	tell	**C**	say	**D**	remember
6	**A**	long	**B**	tall	**C**	high	**D**	large
7	**A**	must	**B**	can	**C**	ought	**D**	would
8	**A**	on	**B**	at	**C**	to	**D**	in
9	**A**	because	**B**	for	**C**	so	**D**	although
10	**A**	short	**B**	small	**C**	tight	**D**	narrow

7 Education

Reading

During the teenage years, many young people can at times be difficult to talk to. They often seem to dislike being questioned. They may seem unwilling to talk about their work in school. This is a normal development at this age, though it can be very hard for parents to understand. It is part of becoming independent, of teenagers trying to be adult while they are still growing up. Young people are usually more willing to talk if they believe that questions are asked out of real interest and not because people are trying to check up on them.

Parents should do their best to talk to their son or daughter about school, work and future plans but should not push them to talk if they don't want to. Parents should also watch for danger signs: some young people in trying to be adult may experiment with sex, drugs, alcohol or smoking. Parents need to watch for any signs of unusual behaviour which may be connected with these and get help if necessary.

1   What is the writer trying to do?

    A   help parents to understand teenagers

    B   give advice to inexperienced teachers

    C   give advice to difficult teenagers

    D   help parents to behave responsibly

2   Why would somebody read the text?

    A   for amusement

    B   for pleasure

    C   for information

    D   for opinion

3   What does the writer say about teenagers?

    A   they enjoy adult relationships

    B   they hate answering questions

    C   they prefer being with their friends

    D   they may behave strangely

4   What does the writer think about parents?

    A   they are not very good listeners

    B   they should make a special effort

    C   they tend to use too much force

    D   they don't understand problems

5 Which is the most suitable picture to go with the text ? Put a tick in the box.

A ☐ B ☐ C ☐ D ☐

Speaking

Look at the photograph. Describe the people and what you think they are doing.

8 Entertainment

Listening

Put a tick in the boxes you think are the most suitable.

1 The art gallery is   **A** ☐ on the first floor.
                               B ☐ at the top of the staircase.
                               C ☐ on the ground floor.
                               D ☐ near the bookshop.

2 Nathalie Howell   **A** ☐ sells books.
                               B ☐ paints pictures.
                               C ☐ takes pictures.
                               D ☐ writes poetry.

3 At 11 am you can listen to   **A** ☐ an orchestra.
                                           B ☐ Russian poetry.
                                           C ☐ children singing.
                                           D ☐ piano playing.

4 Arnie Scott will be   **A** ☐ reading his own poetry.
                                   B ☐ selling books of poems.
                                   C ☐ talking to children.
                                   D ☐ reading short stories.

5 The children's entertainment is for   **A** ☐ 10 and 11 year olds.
                                                       B ☐ children of any age.
                                                      C ☐ parents and children.
                                                       D ☐ children who can act.

6 Visitors can   **A** ☐ see a programme about using video.
                         B ☐ watch video films in a studio.
                         C ☐ help with making a video film.
                         D ☐ listen to a lecture on video.

Writing

You are going to enter an English language competition.

Choose two videos from the pictures below that you would buy for a friend. Then in two paragraphs (about 40 words each) say why you have chosen these two videos for your friend and what you think will be on them.

The winner receives the two videos !

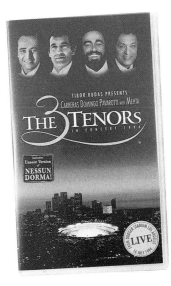 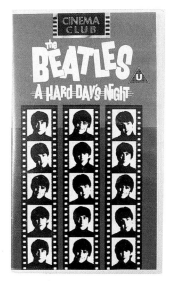 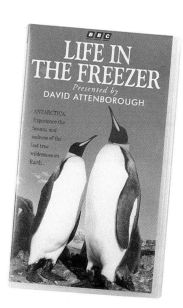

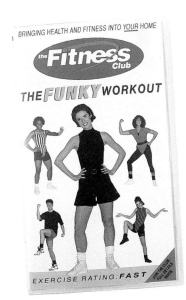 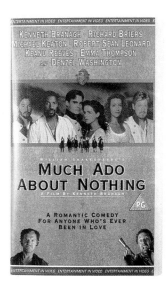 

First choice ....
....

Second choice ....
....

9 Work, Sports, Hobbies

Listening

If you agree with the statement put a tick (✓) under Yes. If you do not agree put a tick under No.

		Yes	No
1	The woman wants to give up playing tennis.	☐	☐
2	She is very good at tennis.	☐	☐
3	The man goes out with his friends during the week.	☐	☐
4	The man suggests having a rest from all sport for a while.	☐	☐
5	The man thinks fishing is an interesting sport.	☐	☐
6	The woman hopes this man will join her each weekend.	☐	☐

Grammar

Here are some sentences about penfriends. Finish the second sentence so that it has the same meaning as the first.

1 Writing letters to penfriends is very common.
 Many ....

2 Some penfriends develop very close relationships.
 Close relationships ....

3 Presents and photographs may be exchanged.
 Some people ....

4 The relationship may last for years.
 The relationship may go ....

5 People can sometimes be disappointed when they meet.
 It ....

UNIT 2 Exercise 23 *Student B*

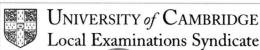

UNIVERSITY *of* CAMBRIDGE
Local Examinations Syndicate

SAMPLE

Candidate Name
If not already printed, write name
in CAPITALS and complete the
Candidate No. grid (in pencil).

Candidate's signature

Examination Title

Centre

Supervisor:

[X] If the candidate is ABSENT or has WITHDRAWN shade here ⊏⊐

Candidate No.

Examination Details

0	0	0	0
1	1	1	1
2	2	2	2
3	3	3	3
4	4	4	4
5	5	5	5
6	6	6	6
7	7	7	7
8	8	8	8
9	9	9	9

PET Reading and Writing - Answer Sheet 1

Reading

Use a pencil.

Mark one letter for each question.

Example:
If you think A is the right answer to the question,
mark your answer sheet like this:

Rub out any answer you want to change, with an eraser.

| 0 | A | B | C | D |

Part 1	Part 2	Part 3	Part 4	Part 5
1 A B C D	6 A B C D E F G H	11 A B	21 A B C D	26 A B C D
2 A B C D	7 A B C D E F G H	12 A B	22 A B C D	27 A B C D
3 A B C D	8 A B C D E F G H	13 A B	23 A B C D	28 A B C D
4 A B C D	9 A B C D E F G H	14 A B	24 A B C D	29 A B C D
5 A B C D	10 A B C D E F G H	15 A B	25 A B C D	30 A B C D
		16 A B		31 A B C D
		17 A B		32 A B C D
		18 A B		33 A B C D
		19 A B		34 A B C D
		20 A B		35 A B C D

Continue on the other side of this sheet

Writing (Parts 1 and 2)

Write your answer clearly in the space provided.

SAMPLE

Part 1: Write your answers below.	Do not write here
1	1
2	2
3	3
4	4
5	5

Part 2: Write your answers below.	Do not write here
6	6
7	7
8	8
9	9
10	10
11	11
12	12
13	13
14	14
15	15

Put your answer to Writing Part 3 on Answer Sheet 2 ⟶

UNIVERSITY *of* CAMBRIDGE
Local Examinations Syndicate

SAMPLE

Candidate Name
If not already printed, write name
in CAPITALS and complete the
Candidate No. grid (in pencil).
Candidate's signature

Examination Title

Centre

Supervisor:

[X] If the candidate is ABSENT or has WITHDRAWN shade here ▭

Candidate No.

Examination Details

0	0	0	0
1	1	1	1
2	2	2	2
3	3	3	3
4	4	4	4
5	5	5	5
6	6	6	6
7	7	7	7
8	8	8	8
9	9	9	9

PET Listening Answer Sheet

• You must transfer all your answers from the Listening Question Paper to this answer sheet.

Use a pencil

For Parts 1,2 and 4: Mark one letter for each question.

For example, if you think A is the right answer to
the question, mark your answer sheet like this:

0

Change your answer
like this:

For Part 3: Write your answers in the spaces
next to the numbers (14 - 19) like this:

0 *example*   ▭ 0 ▭

	Part 1		Part 2		Part 3	Do not write here		Part 4
1	A B C D	8	A B C D	14		▭ 14 ▭	20	A B
2	A B C D	9	A B C D	15		▭ 15 ▭	21	A B
3	A B C D	10	A B C D	16		▭ 16 ▭	22	A B
4	A B C D	11	A B C D	17		▭ 17 ▭	23	A B
5	A B C D	12	A B C D	18		▭ 18 ▭	24	A B
6	A B C D	13	A B C D	19		▭ 19 ▭	25	A B
7	A B C D							

PET-L

DP312/86

Acknowledgements

I am indebted to a number of people who have been instrumental in shaping this book. I would especially like to thank Sue Garvin (The British Institute, Florence) for her unfailingly constructive criticism and suggestions, and also Mike Rogers (English 1, Seville), Matthew Hancock, and Charlie Pickthall (Abon Language School, Bristol) for their valuable comments and willingness to try out the materials.

Finally, my grateful thanks to Howard who has refrained from cleaning the study so that I could find everything, and Dominic and Xanthé who have remained tolerant and self-sufficient.

The publishers would like to thank the following for permission to reproduce copyright material. They have tried to contact all copyright holders, but in cases where they may have failed will be pleased to make the necessary arrangements at the first opportunity.

Texts:

Mrs T Addison, Helston 101; Amnesty International 69; Badgerline 11; The Barbican Centre – John Macneill, 75, 77; Birmingham Royal Ballet 74; Boak House, Coverak 101; The Bristol Hippodrome 83, 84; British Airways 125, 127; British Gas 29; British Rail 58, 59; Business Design Centre 74, 76; Café Matisse, Winchester 38; Cambridge University Press – *A Way With Maths* – Nigel Langdon and Charles Snape 72; The Countryside Commission 95; Cresta Holidays 56; The Cricketers, Winchester 38; Crossroads Motel, Redruth 101; Department of Social Security 69; Department of Transport 11; Donaldsons 15; Early Times 9, 49, 66, 73, 82, 88, 89, 90; English Heritage 74; English National Ballet 84; Evening Standard 82; Naomi Games 32; Glenbracken House, Portreath 101; Great Western Train Company Ltd 117; The Green Party 69; The Indy 63; Kenwood 75, 77; Lake District National Park Authority 95; Loughborough University of Technology 68; The Midweek Journal, Somerset 29; Mounts Bay House Hotel, Cornwall 101; The Museum of London 74, 77; The Museum of the Moving Image – Marilyn Monroe © VIP/Captain Scarlet © ITC Entertainment Group Ltd/Muppets © Henson Associates, Inc 75, 77; National Express 58; The National Gallery 75, 77; The National Motor Museum, Beaulieu 12; Nestlé, Switzerland 106; The New York Pizza Company, Winchester 38; The Penmenner House Hotel, Cornwall 101; Polcoverack Farm, Coverack 101; Radio Times 80; The Rajpoot Tandoori Restaurant, Salisbury 38; The Retreat, Perranporth 101; Royal Mail Parcelforce 103; Royal National Theatre – Daniil Kharms 74, 77; Sadler's Wells Theatre 74, 77; J Sainsbury Plc 33, 39; Schweizerhof, Bern 58; Somerset County Library 69; The State House, Lands End 34, 122; The Theatre Royal, Bath 85; Thomas Cook 29; Thomson City Breaks 56; Tourauto, Ware 56; University Arms, Cambridge 58; Watches of Switzerland Ltd 112; Welsh National Opera 83; The White Horse Hotel, Salisbury 38.

Dictionary extracts are taken from the *Collins COBUILD Essential English Dictionary.*

Photographs:

Ace Photo Agency 36, 62, 71; Adams Picture Library 87, 97; Allsport (UK) Ltd 97, 108; Art Directors Photo Library 43; Aspect Picture Library Ltd 46, 50(c); Aviation Picture Library 61; Anthony Blake 122; Gareth Boden Photography 74-5, 90, 98, 122, 129, 131; Stuart Boreham 61; Camera Press 71; J Allan Cash Ltd 17, 87, 117; The Central Office of Information – Department of Education and Science 129; Cephas Picture Library 46, 122; Colorsport 97; Cresta Holidays 56; Shirley Curran – The International School of Geneva 70; The Early Times 9, 49, 73; Greg Evans Photo Library 40; Format Partners Photo Library 122; Howard Fried-Booth 26, 81; Sally and Richard Greenhill 87; Susan Griggs Agency Ltd 6, 22, 36(b), 55, 86, 101; Robert Harding Picture Library 6, 17, 22, 36(c), 40, 46, 62; Michael Holford 50(a), (b), (d); The Hulton Picture Company 72(c); The Hutchison Library 50(e), 62; The Image Bank 6, 22, 36(a), 55, 61, 62, 70, 86, 93; Images Colour Library 22, 70; Impact Photos 36(e), 71; The Indy 63; Raymond Irons 79; The Kobal Collection 80; Leeds City Council 26; London Features International Ltd 72(a), 89; Loughborough University of Technology 68; David Muscroft Photography and Picture Library 80; The National Motor Museum, Beaulieu 12; The Natural History Photographic Agency 87; North-West Tourist Board 40; P.G.L. Young Adventure Ltd 22, 55, 62, 71; Picturepoint Ltd 6, 22, 55, 86; Popperfoto 88; Rex Features Ltd 40, 72(b), (d), (f), 80; Royal Mail Parcelforce 103; Shardwick Communications 125; Frank Spooner Pictures 72(e); The State House 34; Tony Stone Images 46, 101, 122, 132; Janine Wiedel 70, 71; World Pictures 56.

All other photographs by Mark Harrison

Illustrations:

Joan Corlass; Mark Doherty; Richard Draper; Leo Duff; Antonia Enthoven; Alison Everitt; Leo Hartas; Gordon Hendry; Carl Melegari; Sebastian Quigley; Mark Thomas; Sue Walliker; Tracey Wilson

Pearson Education Limited
Edimburgh Gate Harlow
Essex CM20 2JE England
and Associated Companies throughout the world.
www.longman-elt.com

First edition © HarperCollins Publishers Limited 1991
This edition © Addison Wesley Longman Limited 1996

Tenth impression 2001

Set in 10.5/13pt Garamond Light

Printed in Spain
by Gráficas Estella, S. A.

ISBN 0 17 557119 8